THIS BOOK BELONGS TO

_____

PREPARE TO WIN

Disclaimer

While the publisher and authors have used their best efforts in preparing this book, they make no representations or warranties with respect to the accuracy or completeness of the contents of this book and specifically disclaim, to the extent permitted by applicable law including the Australian Consumer Law, all warranties of any kind, express or implied, including, but not limited to, implied warranties of merchantability, title, non-infringement and fitness for a particular purpose.

The material in this publication, including but not limited to advice, methods and strategies is of the nature of general comment only, and does not represent professional advice. It may not be suitable for your situation. You should consult with a professional where appropriate. The publisher and the authors make no guarantees concerning the level of success you may experience by following the advice, methods and strategies contained in this publication. Neither the publisher nor authors shall be liable for any loss of profit or any other commercial damages, including but not limited to special, incidental, consequential, or other damages for any person taking or not taking action based on the information in this publication.

Orders of magnitude and information about consulting companies are based on authors' experience and research but they may not be accurate, reliable or up to date.

Popular companies were sometimes selected to exemplify a business concept or illustrate a business case study. However, case studies and examples in this book were designed for educational purposes only. All statements related to these companies, including but not limited to, company strategy, products, footprint, operations, staff, financials and specific context elements are fictional. Any resemblance to actual companies or events is thus purely coincidental.

All brand names and product names used in this book are trademarks, registered trademarks, or trade names of their respective holders. STRATINTERVIEWS is not associated with any product or vendor in this book.

ISBN 978-0-6450011-0-5 (paperback)

A catalogue record for this work is available from the National Library of Australia

Design: STRATINTERVIEWS
Cover & Sections Artwork: Pierre Burnel
Diagrams: Authors
Icons: © M.Style/Adobe Stock
Pictures: © iStock.com

Published by:
STRATINTERVIEWS
P.O. BOX 669
POTTS POINT, NSW 2011
AUSTRALIA
www.stratinterviews.com

PREPARE TO WIN

A COMPREHENSIVE & PRACTICAL GUIDE TO SUCCEED AT STRATEGY INTERVIEWS

VIRGIL BARADEAU
ADELINE CHANEL

JOINING CONSULTING

STRATEGY & FINANCE ESSENTIALS

PROBLEM SOLVING

OTHER KEY DIMENSIONS

APPENDIX

THANK YOU

to our McKinsey, Bain, BCG, Roland Berger, Monitor, Strategy&, L.E.K., ADL, OC&C alumni friends, who kindly shared their perspective and tips, and provided valuable feedback.

WHO IS THIS BOOK FOR?

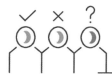

This book is primarily for people keen to join strategy consulting as an intern, associate, consultant or senior consultant.

This includes:

- **MBA degree students and MBA graduates**
- **Undergraduates**
- **Experienced professionals who consider a career shift** after a few years on the "corporate side".

All the business concepts and problem solving tips in this book are, however, valuable for many more people:

- **Consultants** aiming to move to another strategy consulting firm.
- **People willing to join strategy** consulting at a **more senior** level (**Manager, Senior Manager**) and who need a **refresher on specific concepts and case solving techniques.**
- People aiming to join **strategy teams on the "corporate side".**
- To some extent, **people willing to join M&A/Private Equity** firms, or **other types of consulting** (management, IT, HR, etc.).

JOINING STRATEGY IS HARD

MANY PEOPLE WANT TO JOIN STRATEGY CONSULTING...

Every year, a steady flow of undergraduate and graduate students seek employment. In 2018-2019, in the US, 1,968,000 bachelor's degrees and 816,000 master's degrees were conferred[1].

A significant share of them aims to become strategy consultants, especially Business, Engineering and Law graduates. **In Harvard Business School's class of 2020, consulting was the second preferred industry (24%)[2].**

As a matter of fact, some students invest in an MBA primarily to be invited by strategy firms (McKinsey & Co., Boston Consulting Group, Bain & Co. to name the most prestigious ones).

Indeed, for those motivated, strategy consulting offers:

- **Money**: compensation can be substantially higher than in corporate roles.
- **Capabilities:** consultants are exposed to many more business problems than their peers in the industry in a single year. They learn both hard and soft skills and become more versatile.
- **Resume**: a prestigious consulting name on a resume is highly valued by recruiters.
- **Network**: not only do they join a powerful alumni network, but they also build a corporate network with their clients.

...BUT YOU NEED TO GO THROUGH A CHALLENGING PROCESS...

Consultants are the main assets in a consulting firm. Firms pay them well and expect to get a great return on investment by charging clients a high daily rate for their time and effort.

They hope junior consultants will go up the ladder quickly and will increase the scale of the business, overseeing multiple projects and junior teams, again increasing the return on investment they generate.

Firms thus **set the bar high** to identify and recruit switched-on, driven and well-rounded individuals who can take on more and more challenges, year after year.

Sources: 1. nces.ed.gov, 2. www.hbs.edu

Regardless of the firm, interviewers use a combination of case studies and fit or motivation questions to evaluate the candidates':

- **Business acumen:** strategy, corporate finance, ability to sense-check results.
- **Problem solving skills**: ability to structure a problem and to ask the right questions in the right order to get to a logical answer or decision.
- **Quantitative skills**: from basic arithmetic and geometry to more advanced concepts such as analysis, algebra, statistics and probabilities.
- **Consulting knowledge:** how firms operate and which tools, techniques and lingo they use daily.
- **Client-facing readiness**, e.g. poise, resilience, self-awareness, values, etc.

Usually, candidates invited to an interview – about 10% of applications – go through 3 rounds of interviews — including 2 interviews with Partners. The process is sometimes complemented with computer-based business or problem-solving tests, mathematics MCQs and/or group interviews.

IT CAN SOMETIMES GET EVEN HARDER

Strategy consulting is a growing service sector, with a global market size estimated to reach ca. USD 44bn by 2025, growing 5% per year.

It is at the same time a cyclical industry, as the purchase of strategy services by multinational companies is an early indicator of the peaks and troughs they will experience.

Annual recruitment in these firms is thus highly variable. **In tough years – e.g. in COVID-19 times –, recruitment may be frozen or limited to a few roles per office per year**, depending on the local performance.

Source: 3. Kenneth Research – Strategy Consulting Market 2025

PREPARATION IS CRITICAL

Our single hope when we entered the meeting room as interviewers was to **meet someone very smart and nice** that we would really like to bring in our team. In that sense, **both the candidates and us had the same hope: a "yes"** for the next round.

It was, however, extremely frustrating to see many fail because:

- They panicked, and/or
- They had not done their homework.

All invited candidates have great resumes. The challenge for you as a candidate is thus twofold: you must not only do a good job answering questions and solving case studies, but also differentiate yourself from the other candidates. **This cannot be improvised. Thorough preparation is needed.**

The four most common strategy interviewee pitfalls are, in this order:

1. **Lack of structure**: people go down the rabbit hole without having laid out a logical, high-level overview. This applies to both case studies and motivation questions.
2. **Case frameworks**: candidates learn by heart frameworks found online or in books, and try to force-fit case problems. They tend to play back all the framework questions, without any logic to take them from A (a client problem) to Z (a recommendation).

3. **Calculation mistakes**: even PhD's in mathematics fail at basic arithmetic under pressure, when unprepared.
4. **Poor fit**: there are four common archetypes of poor fit candidates:
   a. The "arrogant", who seem to believe they outsmart everyone.
   b. The "indecisive", who hesitate between consulting, banking, Google/Amazon/Facebook/Apple, a digital start-up and a graduate program at a leading FMCG company.
   c. The "cynics", who shamelessly explain they want to join consulting only for a year or two before leaving, and ask whether they can specialize in their preferred industry.
   d. The "idlers", who only enquire about long hours, salary and perks.

Conversely, when asked what made them **successful**, new consultants explain:

"I knew what recruiters were looking for"

"I was confident I could tackle any case study"

"I role-played beforehand to cope with the pressure"

What they have in common is a combination of **competence and confidence**, reached through **significant preparation**. Practically, they went through 3 stages to prepare:

1 **Learn**: they learned how interviewers assess candidates in interviews, and focused on the corresponding core knowledge and techniques.

2 **Practice**: they practiced case studies, quant skills and motivation storytelling to build confidence.

3 **Apply**: they demonstrated, in their application and in each round of interviews, their skills and genuine interest in each specific firm.

HOW CAN THIS BOOK HELP YOU?

We have been through this ourselves. The amount of content available is overwhelming, and everyone will have their preferred book or technique. The correlation with success is not proven and it is all word of mouth.

It is, to say the least, confusing: how to know where to start and who to trust? Which frameworks use? Should you start a case with an SCQ, a MECE tree, or directly a framework?

In addition, **case solving is only one aspect of strategy interview preparation. You also need** to **understand companies** you apply to and practically put together an **application strategy,** optimizing timelines. You need to **tailor** your resume and cover letter and prepare for **motivation** questions. You also need to **practice mathematics**, etc.

You could spend months on each of these elements, researching, refining, and practicing. But you may have an interview scheduled in a few weeks. What should you prioritize? What is a must-have versus a nice-to-have?

This book will be your compass, and the backbone of your preparation to build competence and gain confidence.

It is a **one-stop-shop**, covering all aspects of preparation:

- It will help you **understand your strengths and weaknesses.**
- It will take you on a **practical preparation journey**, step-by-step, from planning to application.
- **It will help you prioritize** your effort (knowledge, practice, research).
- **It summarizes all the essential knowledge** you need to master, presented in a concise, digestible way.
- You will learn the **stress-relieving "solving blocks" case resolution method** – based on how consultants actually solve clients' problems –, which works for 99% of cases.
- It includes a set of **practice exercises and templates** to help you get to grips with the content and the solving blocks method, and fine-tune your storytelling.

NOTE: WHAT THIS BOOK IS NOT ABOUT

The purpose of this book is to give you the essentials to succeed in a strategy interview.
It is not a compendium of all the latest business and consulting concepts and trends.

NAVIGATING THE BOOK

The objective of the book is to cover all the **essentials** to prepare you **to succeed at strategy interviews**, in a very **practical** way.

Depending on your background and experience, we invite you to **adjust the time you dedicate to each section**, from scanning through it to validate you master it all, to reading it multiple times to digest if concepts are new to you.

You will find **cheat sheets, dry runs, quizzes and templates** throughout the book to help you put into practice the key concepts covered and tick all boxes ahead of your interview process.

Here and there, you will find **illustrative examples using familiar companies**.

Core Knowledge

- Pages and sections in this book you cannot overlook when preparing.
  — You will find an overview page 257.
  — If you have very limited preparation time, master the content on these pages before looking at the rest of the content.

Cheat Sheets

- Concise summary of key notions to master:
  — Strategy & Finance Essentials
  — Problem Solving – Starting the case.

- General orders of magnitude to help while sizing and to sense check results.

Homework

- Short exercises to apply key concepts:
  — Strategy & Finance knowledge quiz
  — Problem solving: case dry runs
  — Quant skills dry runs.

- Prep work to list and learn orders of magnitude relevant for your country.

Templates

- Preparation activities pre- and post-interview:
  — Your preparation plan
  — Consulting firm profiling
  — Case study debrief
  — Fit & HR motivation questions
  — Interview tracking.

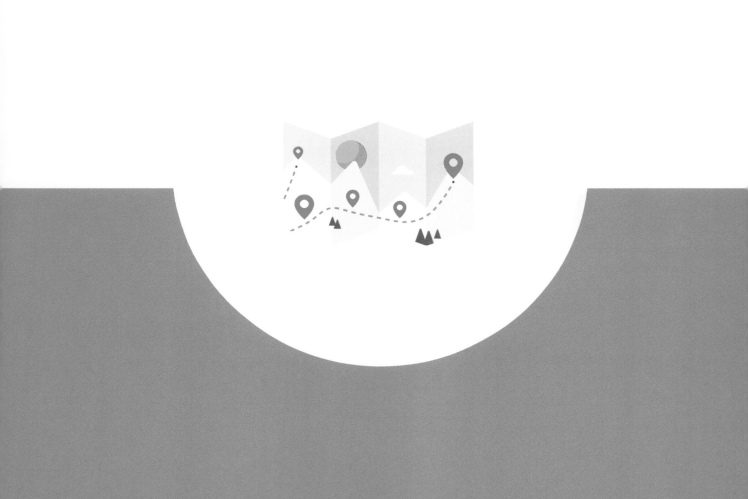

JOINING
CONSULTING

CHAPTER 1
CONSULTING AT A GLANCE
A GLIMPSE BEHIND THE SCENES: HOW STRATEGY FIRMS OPERATE AND RECRUIT

Interviewers will try to assess whether you **know what consulting is**, and whether you have the **right expectations**.

You also need to **understand how they will assess you**, to practice and tick as many boxes as possible in the interview.

This chapter will give you the **essential background knowledge** on:

*   Key strategy **firms** and the **day-to-day processes** in these firms
*   **Recruitment processes** and **competencies** assessed
*   **Two consultant techniques** to master and leverage in case interviews.

KNOW THE RULES OF THE GAME

WHICH STRATEGY FIRMS?

Companies mandate consulting firms to deliver a mission (or engagement).

There is a very large range of engagement types, for instance:

- Corporate & Business Unit Strategy
- M&A due diligences
- Operations review
- Program Management Office (PMO)
- HR & change
- Risk
- IT, etc.

Strategy consulting firms can cover all types of engagements but will primarily focus on the diagnosis and design part – and due diligence projects –, whereas management consultants will usually execute and implement (leading transformations, setting-up PMO, conducting process redesign, etc.).

- Strategy engagements last on average 1-3 months and are fast-paced and intense.
- Management consulting engagements are often longer (>3 months, up to 24 months).

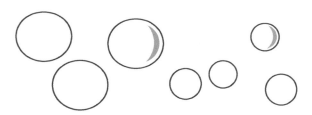

LARGE GENERALISTS ("MBB")	STRATEGY PRACTICES IN LARGE PROFESSIONAL SERVICES FIRMS	MID-SIZE GENERALISTS	MID-SIZE SPECIALISTS
• McKinsey & Co. (McK) • Boston Consultig Group (BCG) • Bain & Co.	• Strategy& (PwC) • Monitor Deloitte • EY-Parthenon • KPMG Strategy • Accenture Strategy	• L.E.K. Consulting • Oliver Wyman • Roland Berger Strategy Consultants • Kearney • Arthur D. Little • ...	• Simon-Kucher & Partners (Pricing) • ZS Associates (Life Sciences) • PA Consulting (Digital) • ...
Historically focused on business, corporate and public sector strategy. Can also deliver operations, digital, IT engagements.	Strategy players acquired in the 2010s to provide end-to-end – strategy to implementation – services. Strategy practices remain relatively independent.	Global players primarily focused on business and corporate strategy.	Global players recognized for their functional or sector expertise.

Note: there are, in addition, a handful of high-calibre strategy boutiques in each market worth looking into.

BEHIND THE SCENES: HOW CONSULTING WORKS
KEY BUSINESS PROCESSES

Go-to-market: raising company awareness, identifying clients' needs, offering services through a proposal.

Staffing & delivering projects: building a team with people available and managing the end-to-end project.

Finance: controlling project financials to maintain profitability targets.

Recruitment: recruiting consultants and partners to maintain a balanced pyramid.

Training: informal and formal training sessions to learn hard and soft skills.

Performance reviews: evaluation of consultants and decisions on compensation and promotion.

BEHIND THE SCENES: HOW CONSULTING WORKS
GO-TO-MARKET

PROJECT PROPOSALS

Consultants write **proposals** to offer their services to clients, based on the discussions they had with them. This can be a competitive or non-competitive process.

The proposal itself is usually a PowerPoint document (though some public sector clients will require lengthy Word proposals with annexes). The blocks outlined on the next page are usually covered and can be configured in different ways.

As a consultant, you will likely be asked to help research information and build, "sanitize" (anonymize) or format slides for Partners and Managers, usually when you are not staffed on a project (when you are "on the beach/on the bench").

MARKETING

Beyond proposals, the firm leadership team aims to raise the firm's profile on the market around specific topics, with viewpoint publications released online and advertised in the media.

You may be asked to help with research and with drafting these while on the bench.

KEY PROPOSAL BLOCKS

CONTEXT & OBJECTIVES	• Key **context** elements known or shared by the client • **Problem** statement and project **objectives**.

PROPOSED APPROACH	• Key **learnings/success factors** from previous experience
	• **Approach overview** (one page mapping phases over time)
	• **Deep-dive by phase**:
	  — Activities (e.g. workshop, interviews, modeling design and build)
	  — Outputs/deliverables (and illustrations)
	  — Methodologies, frameworks or tools used.

WORKPLAN	• **Gantt chart** mapping key activities, deliverables and governance meetings (core team and steering team).
TEAM	• **Team** structure diagram • **1-page resumes** (at least leadership team and project manager).
CREDENTIALS	• **"Why 'Insert firm name here'?":** — 3-5 arguments relevant for this project.

FEES	• Depending on the project complexity and client's needs, 4 main commissioning models exist:
	  — **Fixed fee** (most common): a scope of work – SoW –, including timelines is defined, with a predefined cost.
	  — **Time and materials**: a daily rate is agreed for each level of seniority. Clients can flexibly decide the level of support and get billed for days used (plus expenses). This is essentially a contractor model.
	  — **Retainer** (less frequent): clients basically pay a monthly or quarterly fee to make sure they can have access to qualified resources when needed.
	  — **Value-based/Risk-sharing**: these are usually structured as a flat fee plus an "at risk" fee.
	  The latter is paid if performance metrics (KPIs) defined upfront are met. It is challenging for strategy work, where the actual implementation of recommendations can take months or years to materialize, making the definition and review of KPIs tricky.
	• Additional **expenses**: travel and hospitality costs, printing... usually billed at cost, with a % of fees as a cap.

BEHIND THE SCENES: HOW CONSULTING WORKS
PROJECT STAFFING AND DELIVERY

ONCE SOLD, THE TYPICAL PROJECT STEPS ARE:

1 STAFFING

- The Manager and Partner review consultants' availability and try to set-up a team that meets the project needs and that is as close as possible to the team member profiles outlined in the proposal.

2 INTERNAL TEAM KICK-OFF

- The Manager and Partner brief the team on the project objectives and set roles and expectations.
- The team aligns on team norms and preferences, e.g. working hours, style.
- The team generates hypotheses — see issue tree analysis page 34.

3 INITIAL STORYLINING

- These form the backbone of the final recommendation.
- The team prepares a mock-up deliverable to identify analyses to conduct.

4 INITIAL WORKPLAN AND WORK ALLOCATION

- The project manager delineates analyses and workstreams and assigns them to team members.
- A workplan is put together and shared with clients for upfront alignment on timelines and expectations. It is then used to track delivery vs. plan.

5 KICK OFF WITH CLIENTS

- The team aligns on the approach with the client.
- Initial hypotheses and planned analysis are tested.
- A data request is issued (e.g. financiels, HR data...).
- Governance is agreed and set-up (e.g. Core Team progress updates and Steering Committee meetings).
- Other stakeholder engagement forums are scheduled (e.g. interviews, workshops).

6 INTERIM DELIVERABLES PRODUCTION

- The team delivers on the analytical plan (e.g. desktop research, interviews, data analysis, modeling, etc.).
- Team members check-in/check-out on a daily basis to share progress and tackle roadblocks.
- The team produces slides to summarize insights.

7	STEERING COMMITTEES (STEERCO)	• The team provides a progress update, outlining key milestones and risks. • Key insights since the kick-off or the previous SteerCo are shared. • The Steering team makes key decisions needed for the team to progress.
8	RECOMMEN-DATION	• The team prepares the final deliverable. • It prewires key stakeholders a few days before the final Steering Committee to ensure full buy-in. • Recommendations are presented to the Steering Committee.
9	WRAP-UP	• Deliverables are finalized post Steering Committee. • Sources or models requested by the clients are consolidated and shared.

SUPPORT

Some firms have support services team, helping consultants with:

- Design services to create illustrations or format slides
- Research services (usually desktop research)
- Subject Matter Experts (SME) panels
- Modeling services
- Digital development support.

LIFESTYLE

Being a consultant means being flexible:

- **Workload goes through peaks** – long nights for a long period of time, sometimes weekends – **and troughs** — at times hardly anything to do. Fully enjoy troughs to do things you did not have time to do during peak times.
- **Travel** may be required and depending on the client and partner, on-site presence might be requested. You will quickly discover how to become a proficient business traveler and how to carve out time to visit cities you travel to.

BEHIND THE SCENES: HOW CONSULTING WORKS
OTHER KEY PROCESSES

FINANCE

To meet profit targets and manage cash flow, Partners and Managers watch carefully:

- **Price points (daily rates) and project gross margin**:
  — Clients usually ask for a discount but this directly impacts net margin.
     This is accepted only as an investment when building relationships or when there is a significant volume of projects every year.
  — The gross margin is normally set to be highest for juniors and lowest for Partners.
     Consequently, too much senior time on the project is not only limiting the junior budget but also decreasing the project margin.

- **Billing**: payment upon project completion is avoided as much as possible. Proposals thus usually mention a specific billing cycle. Common billing models are:
  — Billing upon completion of key phases
  — For small projects: 50% upfront, 50% at the end
  — For larger projects: billing on a monthly basis

- **Expense payments**: expenses must be documented with receipts and approved by Partners or Managers and Finance in a timely manner to be billed to the client.

- **Timesheets**: some firms ask consultants to track the time they spend on projects – e.g. recordings half-days – to be able to track the profitability of projects. It can help with billing as well, e.g. for a retainer.

RECRUITMENT (SEE DEEP-DIVE IN NEXT SECTION)

Firms usually have a Human Resources team with people in charge of recruitment, as well as a pool of recruiters (**Senior Consultants and above**):

- HR usually take care of screening CVs, contacting you and scheduling interviews.
- Recruiters allocate a few hours every week to run interviews. They then share their feedback with the HR team, which follows-up with you.

TRAINING

Most of the real learning happens in projects. However, most firms put in place training days or weeks, in the office or in off-sites with other offices, to train consultants on hard and soft skills and to enable cross-office networking.

PERFORMANCE REVIEWS

At the end of each project, managers evaluate consultants and provide feedback in a feedback session.

Evaluations are consolidated and usually summarized – by the consultant's mentor – for mid-year or end-of-year performance review meetings.

Consultants are tiered, leading to specific compensation levels. Performance reviews are also the opportunity to decide on promotions and identify specific development areas.

RECENT TRENDS

Target skill sets have started shifting, with now a **new interest** in candidates with:

- **Agile** development capabilities
- **User Experience** skills
- **Data science** backgrounds (for automation and artificial intelligence solutions)
- **Experience in startups.**

Cybersecurity is becoming the highest growth area for firms involved in risk advisory.

Firms have also started increasing their **venture model**, taking stakes in promising startups and providing them with their expertise and an access to their network.

HOW FIRMS RECRUIT
RECRUITMENT CHANNELS

Consulting firms rely on five main channels to recruit candidates:

1 The standard process is to receive applications **online** (via firm's recruitment interfaces).

2 Firms collect many resumes on **recruitment fairs**. This is usually equivalent to applying online. The consultant can add a sign or comment on the resume to help the screening team select or discard the profile (based on how you interacted, your questions, etc.).

3 Firms organize **campus events** (e.g. business case challenges, presentations...) to increase or maintain their brand equity and identify some relevant profiles.

4 Consultants can also **recommend** someone internally. This can help candidates with a profile that would otherwise be considered "average" in the standard application process.

5 Last but not least, firms pay **headhunters** to source experienced candidates (Senior Consultants and above) when a specific expertise is sought or when there is a need to bolster a level in the pyramid.

The **standard process** is in theory designed to take you into the pipeline if the firm considers you meet their target criteria. It should thus be the **default approach**. Keep in mind, however, that you cannot apply twice in a short period of time as companies would expect a significant upside in your resume to consider inviting you.

An **internal recommendation** is, however, the **most efficient approach** to get invited:

- Leveraging someone you know...
- ... Or directly contacting consultants (e.g. alumni from your school) to gather information and ask for their support. Note that most firms have put in place incentives programs to reward consultants recommending candidates obtaining and accepting an offer.

Recruitment fairs are a good opportunity to gather additional information on the company, and getting feedback from junior consultants on their experience. It is, however, **difficult to stand out** and if you are stressed or unprepared, you can easily look silly. If you decide to meet consultants, come with a robust resume, have a clear list of relevant questions and **be prepared to introduce yourself in front of a group** (other students listen to you and to the consultants' answers).

Events organized by firms can give you a good exposure and fast-track your entry into the pipeline. It should, however, be in addition to the traditional channels, considering the limited frequency and reach of these events.

RESUME SCREENING LOGIC

It is not unusual for a local office to receive more than a hundred resumes in a week to screen. It is thus critical to make yours compelling and differentiating.

Recruitment teams usually do an **initial sort** based on curricula and experience criteria, e.g.:

MBA STUDENTS/GRADUATES

- Do our clients (or our firm) recognize and **value this MBA**?
- Are previous education/companies/functions **relevant to our clients or our projects**?
- Did the candidate work for a **professional services company** (e.g. management consulting, financial advisory, law, audit), which would share some **skills similarity** with strategy firms?

OTHER CANDIDATES

Is the candidate from a target school?

Yes

- Do they seem to **tick core skills** (e.g. problem solving, structure, languages) and credentials (e.g. GMAT >700)?
- Did they try to do **more than the average** at school — either through competitive internships or co-curricular activities with responsibilities?

No

- Does the candidate have a relevant work experience that would suggest they have some of the **core strategy skills** — e.g. internship in a recognized strategy or management consultancy, PE, M&A or Venture Capital firm?
- Has the candidate another work experience or **skill** that could be **new/missing in the firm** today but important for future projects, and that would suggest they have either:
  — **Strong logic/analytical skills**, e.g. data science, machine learning, blockchain knowledge?
  — **Business acumen/resourcefulness** e.g. start-up creation, digital marketing?

INITIAL SORT

YES   **MAYBE**   **NO**

Recruiters then quickly scan YES's and MAYBE's **cover letters** to confirm the initial sort.

They make a **final call** on the number of people **entering the recruitment pipeline or put on hold**, based on their projected needs and average interview success rate.

- As a rule of thumb, **1 candidate out of 10 resumes is invited.** Of these, **1 in 10 will get an offer**.
- Note: criteria are more or less stringent depending on the period of the year — if you apply at peak times, it may be more competitive.

HOW FIRMS RECRUIT
CLASSIC RECRUITMENT PROCESS

Historically, the standard recruitment process used to consist in 6 interviews (3 rounds of 2 interviews):

- Round 1: Senior Consultants or Managers
- Round 2: Managers, Principals or Directors
- Round 3: Partners (sometimes Managing Partner) or Associate Partners.

APPLICATION	PRELIMINARY PROCESS	ROUND NO.1	ROUND NO.2	ROUND NO.3	
• Resume • Cover Letter	• HR interview • Logic/math test	• Interview no.1 • Interview no.2	• Interview no.3 • Interview no.4	• Interview no.5 • Interview no.6	Offer?
Profile screening	(Optional)	Case studies with consultants			

▶ GO/NO GO decision by the recruitment team (HR and/or consultants met)

Each interview usually lasts one hour. Most of the time it is primarily dedicated to a **case study** (40-45 minutes). It also covers the following:

- **Short intro** from the interviewer (2-3 minutes).
- **Fit/motivation questions** (5-10 minutes) to better understand who you are and why you want to join consulting and this firm in particular.
- A bit of time – often at the end of the interview – to answer **general questions** the candidate may have, e.g. on the firm, the role, the type of projects, etc.

TYPICAL STRATEGY INTERVIEW FORMATS

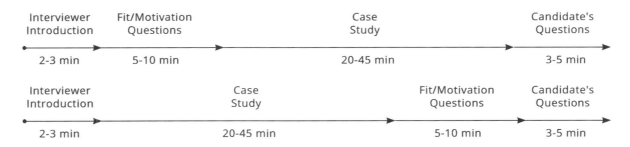

FIRM/OFFICE-SPECIFIC PROCESS TWEAKS

Each firm – and to some extent local office – regularly tailors this process to maximize its effectiveness, considering vacancies and recruiters' capacity. They can leverage a few levers to do this.

The first lever used is implementing a **cost-effective first round filtering**, e.g.:

- Some firms start the process with a computer-based test, online or on premises, which assesses problem-solving skills, logic, business sense and to some extent creativity and psychology, e.g.: McKinsey Problem Solving Test (PST), BCG Potential test.
- Others filter on quantitative skills (e.g. Oliver Wyman online numerical reasoning test).

The second lever is to **reduce the time spent with candidates**, e.g.:

- Replace – like some McKinsey offices – the first round of interviews by a short phone interview with a short case study, much more flexible than a 1h face-to-face interview.
- Reduce the number of rounds or the number of interviews per round — usually when there are strong recruitment needs.
- Ask candidates to prepare a paper-based case study and present insights and recommendations to the interviewer in a shorter face-to-face meeting.

The third lever is to **condense the whole interview process**, e.g.:

- Oliver Wyman proposed in some offices the 1-day process, leading to job offers at the end of the day for successful candidates (powerful to be ahead of other firms with longer processes).
- Monitor historically had a group interview to evaluate the collaboration dynamics and to run multiple interviews in a day.

REGARDLESS OF THE FIRM AND OF THE INTERVIEW PROCESS, ALL INTERVIEWERS ASSESS SIMILAR COMPETENCIES (SEE DETAILS ON THE FOLLOWING PAGE).

HOW FIRMS RECRUIT
COMPETENCIES ASSESSED

1	2	3	4	5
PROBLEM SOLVING	**BUSINESS ACUMEN**	**QUANT SKILLS**	**CONSULTING KNOW-HOW**	**CLIENT-FACING READINESS**

Interviewers try in the interview to:

- Get the best understanding possible of your **strengths and weaknesses** in a limited amount of time.
- **Benchmark you** vs. previous candidates and other candidates applying in parallel.
- Evaluate the **investment that will be required** to fill some of your gaps if the firm hires you (no one is perfect).

Each firm has its own assessment grid. But all roughly cover these 5 competency buckets:

1. **Business Acumen**
2. **Problem Solving**
3. **Quant Skills**
4. **Consulting Know-How**
5. **Client-facing readiness.**

You thus need to work on these dimensions to:

- Not give the stick to be beaten.
- Differentiate vs. other applicants.

---

1 PROBLEM SOLVING

Problem solving is at the heart of the interview. There is no right or wrong answer, but you have to successfully manage the case study to go to the following round.

A strong case study indicates that you know how to **listen**, **structure** a problem, **ask** questions, **integrate input** into your thinking, **calculate** properly and **summarize** your recommendation.

Solving a case study with an interviewer should be interesting. It is the opportunity to experience what your life in this consulting firm could look like. If you enjoy solving a problem with your interviewer, it is likely you will like working in a consulting team.

However, **solving case studies requires preparation**. You need to come to the interview with a strong understanding of what a case study is, what the different types of case studies are, and of how to solve them. **Once you master the method, practice will be key** to come prepared and confident.

2 BUSINESS ACUMEN

Interviewers will expect you to have a minimum level of "business sense" during the interview, which will help you grab concepts quickly, make assumptions and challenge your results in the case study. This encompasses **corporate and business strategy**, and key **corporate finance** concepts.

Having in mind a wide range of **orders of magnitude** (e.g. population or number of households, price of a kWh, annual revenue of Apple, height of the tallest building in the world, etc.) will help you demonstrate that you are not out of touch with reality.

3 QUANT SKILLS

During the case study, the interviewer will test your calculation skills. He/she can ask you to calculate a loss, a revenue increase, size a market or calculate how many encounters are required for a player to win a tennis tournament.

Performing calculations in front of someone is totally different from calculating on your own, with plenty of time. For many candidates, it becomes the most **stressful** moment of the interview.

In most cases, calculations are "simple" (e.g. basic arithmetic, percentage) and **can be performed mentally** or with a pen and paper. It happens, though, that interviewers decide to test your quantitative capabilities more thoroughly, usually to assess to which extent you could be assigned to a highly quantitative project. In that case, performing well on advanced mathematics (e.g. algebra, analysis, statistics and probability) will give you extra points. Not succeeding at these would unlikely be the sole reason for stopping the recruitment process for you.

4 CONSULTING KNOW-HOW

Interviewers expect candidates to have a minimum **understanding of the consulting world**, i.e. what it is, what the different types of consulting are, who **key consulting firms** are and **how they operate**.

Similarly, you should know what the **day-to-day job of a consultant** is: roles and tasks at the different seniority levels (junior consultant vs. manager vs. partner), how to structure a slide, job lingo.

Showing that you are knowledgeable about the consulting world demonstrates you have a keen interest in this industry and reassures the firm that you know what you are embarking upon.

5 CLIENT-FACING READINESS

Junior consultants are invited to client meetings very quickly. It saves time and it is much more efficient than having a manager repeating everything afterwards. Regardless of the role you are applying to, your ability to **act in a professional manner**, to be a trusted **team player** and your potential to **bring value to the discussion** is also assessed in the interview. The interviewer will test your **resilience and poise**, analyze how you **communicate** and assess your **development potential**.

TWO CONSULTANT TECHNIQUES TO MASTER
"MECE" THINKING AND SOLVING

As a consultant (and as a candidate during the interviews), we will expect you to be "MECE" as much as possible. MECE (Mutually Exclusive, Collectively Exhaustive, usually pronounced "mee-see") describes a way to list a set of concepts or questions that cover the full topic, without overlapping.

E.g. Water can occur in three states: liquid, solid, or gas.

Building on the MECE principle, you can **break down a problem** into more precise (likely simpler) sub-questions or underlying drivers. Doing this several times allows you to build an **issue tree**.

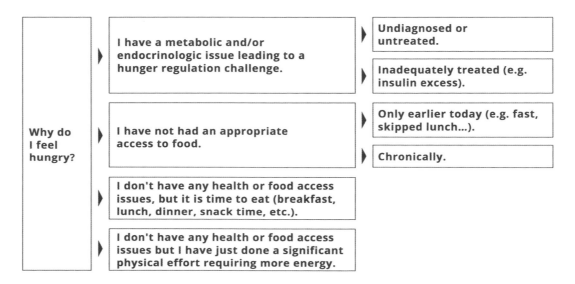

In the simple example above, the list of potential causes seems to cover probably 95% of causes of hunger (sufficiently exhaustive list) and they are all distinct hypotheses, which can be tested independently.
Note: this issue tree can be developed into many more levels, depending on the level of granularity required.

Consultants leverage the issue tree to **allocate work** to team members and to **draft "the story"** at the beginning of the project with a set of **hypothetical key messages**. As supporting analyses are run, the story evolves and the final recommendation takes its final shape. **It is a very effective way to focus consultants' efforts and to manage tight timelines.**

Being MECE is critical: it will help you pull together a compelling resume and cover letter, and will help you logically structure your case study approach.

EXECUTIVE COMMUNICATION

You will often hear about "**Executive Summaries**" (including in this book).

An Executive Summary – or "Exec. Sum." – usually takes the form of **one page with plain bullet points and sub-bullet points**, included at the beginning of a key presentation or final report.

Consultants believe that the most effective way to communicate messages to clients and Executives is to **present first the higher-level insights or takeaways**, before detailing the underlying rationale.

Clients can thus have a grasp of the whole presentation, reading a single page.

To build these, consultants apply a **similar method[1] to the MECE issue tree**:

- They list first the few **critical messages** to remember (usually 3-5). They are ideally recommendations or decisions to be made.
- Then, they write under each message the key **supporting insights or context elements** explaining the bullet point above.

1. Consultants sometimes refer to this technique as **"The Pyramid Principle"** — a book by Barbara Minto on the topic of logical writing, thinking and problem solving.

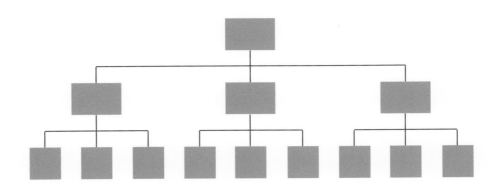

You will finish the interview on a high note if you are able to wrap-up the case study by summarizing the key points, following the pyramid principle approach.

CHAPTER 2
YOUR PREP PLAN
STRATEGICALLY PLANNING YOUR APPLICATIONS AND INTERVIEW PREPARATION

Success in interviews requires both competence and confidence.

The two are interdependent and will come by:

- Mastering the core fundamental business concepts.
- Being comfortable using the Solving Blocks method to tackle any case study.
- Knowing you will not make a calculation mistake.
- Practicing, with friends and with people you don't know, to learn how to cope with stress.
- Having a clear compelling story to show your motivation.

Unless you have a recent consulting experience, **preparing for these interviews takes time (easily 2 to 3 months).**

However, firms can process your application in a few days (in an off-peak period) and invite you for a first round 2 weeks after your application. You should thus **wait as much as possible before applying** to be sufficiently prepared.

We will give you some tips in this chapter to help you **map out your application and preparation roadmap.**

PREPARE
EARLY

APPLY
LATE

COMPREHENSIVE PREPARATION SEQUENCE

While firms acknowledge diverse profiles are valuable for them, the core set of expectations is very similar for all candidates applying at a certain level, regardless of their background. We have outlined below a logical preparation sequence. In crafting your preparation plan (see page 44), you will need to decide how much time you need to spend on each item below.

ASAP (DEDICATE ~ 1-2 MONTH(S) IF YOU HAVE NO BUSINESS EXPERIENCE)

MILESTONES

LEARN

- **Business Acumen:**
  — It is all about value (p54)
  — Business Strategy (p64)
  — Corporate Strategy (p108)
  — Valuation (p118)
- **Knowledge Quiz** (p126)

- **Solving Blocks** case study resolution method (p136)
- **Case dry runs** homework (p192)

- **Required quant skills** and dry runs (p224)
- Personal list of **orders of magnitude** (p220)

PRACTICE

- **Calculations under time pressure:**
  — Maths questions
  — Quantitative business problems (GMAT-like)

APPLY

- Prioritize firms and conduct initial **profiling** (p48)

- Write **resume and cover letter** (p46)

If you are joining a process via a headhunter, you will likely be invited for a first round of interviews within 2-3 weeks. In this case you critically need to **prioritize items below**, probably focusing on the case solving method and motivation. Make sure you also **master the core knowledge** (see overview page 257).

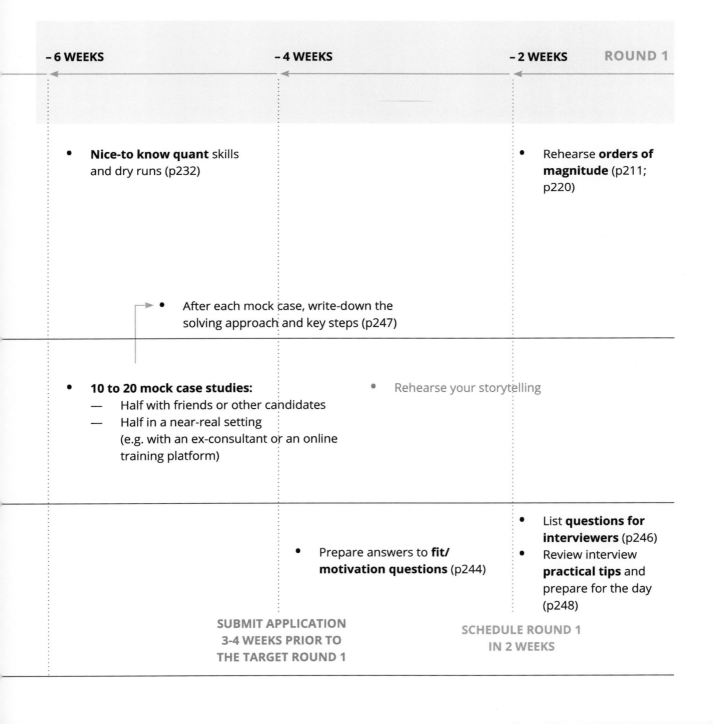

– 6 WEEKS   – 4 WEEKS   – 2 WEEKS   ROUND 1

- **Nice-to know quant** skills and dry runs (p232)

- Rehearse **orders of magnitude** (p211; p220)

- After each mock case, write-down the solving approach and key steps (p247)

- **10 to 20 mock case studies:**
  — Half with friends or other candidates
  — Half in a near-real setting (e.g. with an ex-consultant or an online training platform)

- Rehearse your storytelling

- List **questions for interviewers** (p246)
- Review interview **practical tips** and prepare for the day (p248)

- Prepare answers to **fit/ motivation questions** (p244)

SUBMIT APPLICATION 3-4 WEEKS PRIOR TO THE TARGET ROUND 1

SCHEDULE ROUND 1 IN 2 WEEKS

HOW READY ARE YOU? TAKE THE QUIZ!

		Yes	Unsure	No
1	I can explain in simple terms what corporate strategy is, and how it relates to business unit strategy.	○	○	○
2	I know what the three characteristics of a winning value proposition are.	○	○	○
3	I know what the return on assets tradeoffs are when a company reviews its operating model.	○	○	○
4	I know how to calculate FCFs from financial statements.	○	○	○
5	I know how to calculate the WACC and how to apply the DCF formula.	○	○	○
6	I know how to sequence solving approaches the consultant way, for any case study.	○	○	○
7	I know how a consulting firm operates, and what I will be doing on a daily basis.	○	○	○
8	I have already done case studies as part of a strategy firm recruitment process.	○	○	○
9	I have taken the GMAT in the last 12 months and obtained a score > 700.	○	○	○
10	I have prepared the question: "Why did you not pursue a more prestigious curriculum?"	○	○	○

Total ☐ ☐ ☐

9-10 "Yes"

Congratulations! Your answers suggest you possess the core strategy and finance concepts needed for strategy consulting. You also seem to have done your homework and understand what strategy consulting is about. Practice solving more complex or ambiguous case studies, tailor your storytelling to each firm you interview at, and you will do great!

5-7 "Yes"

Your average score suggests you are on the right track and probably halfway through your preparation. Review areas you marked as "Unsure" or "No" and take the time to fill gaps to be on par with the best candidates. Make sure you master a case study solving method that can be applied to any business problem, to overcome stress during the interviews. Polish as well your storytelling, to highlight your motivation and strengths in a very structured way.

<5 "Yes"

This short quiz shows that you have some fundamental knowledge, know-how and preparation gaps. If you have strategy interviews scheduled soon, consider postponing them by a few weeks to have enough time to get up to speed on core strategy and finance knowledge, consulting know-how, quantitative skills and fit questions preparation. Build in sufficient time to practice case studies and storytelling as well.

HOW MUCH TIME DO YOU HAVE?

YOU MUST MAP OUT YOUR APPLICATION TIMELINE AND WORK BACKWARDS TO IDENTIFY THE OPTIMAL PREPARATION PLAN.

Illustrative

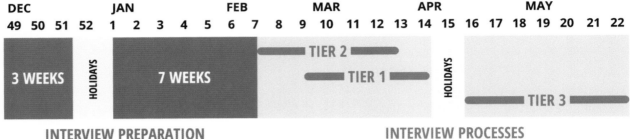

1 PLOT KEY MILESTONES

Define what your **desired job start date** is and plot it on your timeline.

Once you have selected the firms you want to apply to, **clarify their recruitment periods** (check online, ask on campus or call local offices), and plot them on the timeline. Note:

- Even though most companies will say they recruit all year round, in practice, they will often set a recruitment target for the following year and slow-down recruitment once the target is met.
- Some smaller firms operate on a yearly or 6-monthly basis with a new-joiners cohort logic. Recruitment will be organized to build the cohort in time, so applying and joining off-cycle is harder.
- MBA internships must meet very precise recruitment time frames.
- Firms organizing group interviews in their process need enough candidates in the pipeline and will try to avoid interviews in a quiet period (e.g. summer holidays).

2 SEQUENCE APPLICATIONS AND INTERVIEWS

Interviewing in all firms simultaneously is difficult. You should determine which groups of firms you would like to interview at first (considering the recruitment periods).

Three main tactics could be envisaged:

1. Start with the smaller/less prestigious firms to practice before applying to Tier 2/ Tier 1.
2. Do the opposite and start with Tier 1 (e.g. MBBs) and keep others in backup should you fail.
3. Start with Tier 2 firms and shortly afterward apply to Tier 1 ones. Keep Tier 3 ones in backup.

There is no right approach and you should consider:

- The attractiveness of your profile
- Your level of preparation
- Your appetite for risk and whether joining a Tier 1 firm is a must for you.

JUN				JUL				AUG					SEPT				OCT				NOV				
23	24	25	26	27	28	29	30	31	32	33	34	35	36	37	38	39	40	41	42	43	44	45	46	47	48

SUMMER RECRUITMENT PAUSE/SLOWDOWN

HOLIDAYS

◆ **DESIRED JOB START**

Do not worry when defining your sequencing **about having to put on hold an offer** while other processes are ongoing.

Realistically you have a 3-4 weeks window to send your contract signed back, and **you can tell other firms that you need to accelerate the process.**

Recruiters don't like when candidates put them on hold because they know candidates are trying to get an offer in another firm. That being said, it is very unlikely that they withdraw their offer since they thought in the first place that you could be a good addition to their team. They may call you to follow-up though, or invite you for lunch.

3 DERIVE THE TIME AHEAD OF YOU

Our experience is that a **good preparation week requires 4 sessions of 90 minutes during the week, plus 8-10 hours spread over the weekend**. That is a total of **about 15 hours per week**.

Grey out on your timeline any **weeks** that will not be compatible with interview preparation (e.g. exams, internships, holidays...) **and calculate how many "equivalent preparation weeks" you have** ahead of you.

BUILD YOUR DETAILED PREPARATION PLAN

TEMPLATE – WHAT DO YOU NEED TO PREPARE AHEAD OF YOUR FIRST STRATEGY INTERVIEW?

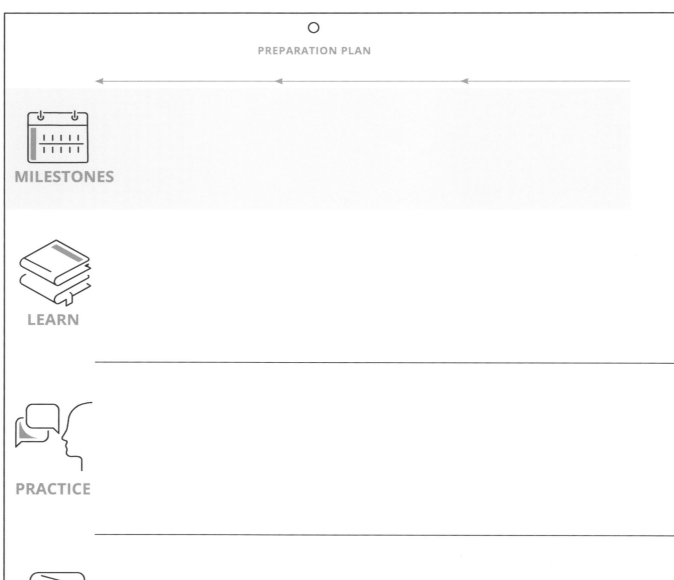

PREPARATION PLAN

MILESTONES

LEARN

PRACTICE

APPLY

WEEKS OR
MONTHS

ROUND 1

CHAPTER 3
RESUME & COVER LETTER
A FEW TIPS TO MAKE YOUR APPLICATION SHINE

You should by now have some visibility on how firms screen and select candidates. You may have realized that **there are some stringent – and to some extent arbitrary – criteria.**

Unfortunately, you can't control these, and you may have limited flexibility to change your "pedigree" to meet firms' screening criteria.

What you can do though, is **make sure that your application demonstrates how great you could be as a consultant**. You should also not give the stick to be beaten.

This chapter will share some **tips to help you** write a consultant-friendly resume and cover letter.

LESS

=

BETTER

PROFILE CONSULTING FIRMS

YOU NEED TO GATHER SOME KEY INFORMATION ABOUT THE FIRMS AND OFFICES YOU CONSIDER APPLYING TO. BUILD A COMPANY PROFILE AND ENRICH IT AS YOU LEARN NEW ELEMENTS, ONLINE, IN INFORMAL CHATS AND DURING INTERVIEWS.

 TEMPLATE

○

CONSULTING FIRM PROFILE

FIRM - OFFICE

MANAGING PARTNER   **NO. EMPLOYEES**   In this office: Worldwide:

KEY INDUSTRIES [LEAD PARTNER]   **MIX OF ENGAGEMENTS**
(Driving most of the revenue)   (Strategy, Org. & Operations, Due Diligences...)

- ...
- ...
- ...

**RECENT
NEWS**   **PEOPLE I KNOW &
KEY INSIGHTS**

- ...   - ...
- ...   - ...
- ...   - ...

WRITING YOUR RESUME

YOUR CV NEEDS TO BE EXTREMELY RELEVANT AND SHARP. THINK ABOUT IT AS AN EXECUTIVE SUMMARY: EVERY SENTENCE SHOULD PROVIDE INSIGHTS INTO WHO YOU ARE AND WHY YOU ARE THE RIGHT FIT.

1 RELEVANT

- **PRIORITIZE** experiences that are relevant. Your summer internship selling shoes when you were 16 and your babysitting experience will not impress consultants. It will actually make them think you can't highlight what matters.
  - If you think secondary experiences are very telling about you, add them to an "Other Experiences" section at the bottom.
- Similarly, prioritize your skills (e.g. programming can in some instances prove helpful in some projects, but listing the 10 coding languages you master or 15 certifications is superfluous).

2 STRUCTURED

- Create clear **MECE BUCKETS,** e.g.:
  - Header with your full name, contact details, work eligibility
  - Work experience (avoid date gaps/inconsistencies; everything should flow simply for the reviewer)
  - Education
  - Other skills (e.g. language, software, relevant tests and certifications, e.g. GMAT, CFA)
  - Publications (if relevant)
  - Hobbies, community involvement, personal achievements.

3 IMPACTFUL

- Describe each experience in a **CONCISE** manner, clearly defining what you did and what was the **IMPACT** (aim for a quantified impact whenever possible), eluding to **CONSULTANT SKILLS.**
- Read again each line and ask yourself: **"IS THIS WORD WORTH IT?"**

4 CLEAN PROFESSIONAL LAYOUT

- **FORMATTING MATTERS**. You want to prove that you can deliver high-quality deliverables and that you spent enough effort and **ATTENTION TO DETAIL** before applying:
  - Create a professional look and feel template.
  - Avoid fancy things, e.g. logos, QR codes, LinkedIn profile link...
  - Check consistency in font type, font size, and style, alignments, margins and spaces. No colors. Use standard fonts.
  - If it is standard to include a photo in a resume in your country, pick a professional one (white background, professional attire, good expression). If your photo is average, do not include it.

5 QUALITY CHECKED

- Print your resume and **REVIEW IT SEVERAL TIMES** to spot issues.
- Ask someone else to review it for you.

WRITING YOUR COVER LETTER

THE COVER LETTER IS NOT ALWAYS READ — YOUR RESUME CAN BE SUFFICIENT. HOWEVER, IF IT IS READ, IT NEEDS TO BE REALLY IMPACTFUL. WRITE IT LIKE AN EXECUTIVE SUMMARY: LESS IS BETTER.

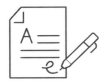

---

1 EXECUTIVE SUMMARY

- Write down first, in bullet points, the **KEY MESSAGES** you want the recruiter to take away after reading your letter:
  — Aim for 3-5 MECE messages.
  — Primarily focus on your relevance for the role, covering:
    ▪ Your core technical skills
    ▪ Your soft skills (e.g. team member, leadership).

- Write then under each bullet point the work experience, achievements or details supporting the key messages:
  — Be consistent with elements you prioritized in your resume.

- This list of bullet points is the outline for your cover letter.

2 WRITE THE CONTENT

- Write the body of your letter, i.e. 3-4 content paragraphs, leveraging your key messages and supporting elements.
  — Use consistent wording between your resume and your cover letter – notably for work experiences – to ease cross-referencing if recruiters seek more details.
  — If you spoke with consultants, mention them in a subtle way.

- Add above a short intro (2-3 lines) to give a succinct overview of where you are today and your interest in the (Senior) Consultant role at firm X:
  — An intro sentence describing the firm is unnecessary. It does not tell the reader anything about you. You can, however, allude to one specificity of the firm to make it not 100% generic.

3 **BUILD THE LETTER**

- Look and feel should be professional obviously:
  — Use the same font and styles as in your resume.
- Add the other typical letter elements (tailored to correspondence standards in your country), e.g.:
  — At the top:
    - Your details as on your resume. Include mobile and email address
    - Application date
    - Recipient details (send to Human Resources, with the company address)
    - An object, e.g. "RE: Application for the full-time Consultant position, starting September 2021".
  — At the bottom:
    - A polite closing, calling for action e.g.:
      "Thank you very much for considering this application. I look forward to hearing from you soon".
    - A complimentary close and your signature, e.g.:
      "Yours faithfully, Jane DOE".

4 **QUALITY CHECK**

- Triple-check typos.
- Check the company name and address. Firms receive way too many letters with a competitor name (we usually reject these applications).
- Print your letter and **REVIEW IT SEVERAL TIMES** to spot issues.
- Ask someone else to review it for you.

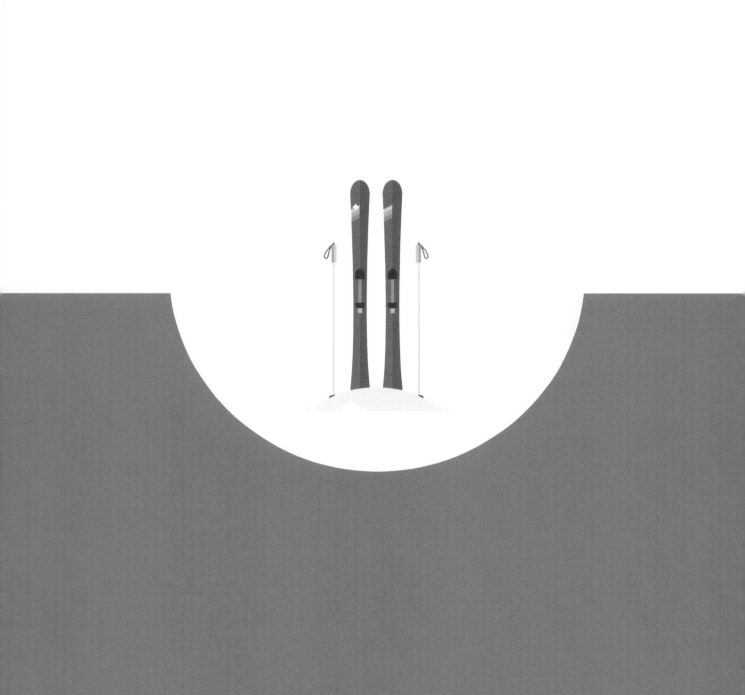

STRATEGY & FINANCE ESSENTIALS

CHAPTER 4
IT IS ALL ABOUT VALUE
DEFINING VALUE AND THE ASSOCIATED CORPORATE FINANCE CONCEPTS

More often than not, **organizations or companies aim to create financial value** acquiring, mobilizing and leveraging assets and ultimately generating even more value. Organizations that don't create value or even worse destroy value are doomed.

Value creation is thus the end game, and **strategy** (which we will cover at length in following chapters), **will aim to maximize value creation over time**.

It is thus critical to define value and **understand the value creation mechanisms**.

In this chapter we will focus on **financial value**, which is the **most common focus of strategy interviews**, and will introduce the **fundamental corporate finance concepts** you need to master, related to financial value.

Note that organizations **also have a corporate social responsibility (CSR)** and can generate short or long-term social and financial value this way, e.g.:

- Large employers in an area can have huge implications on the local economy and create indirect financial and social value.
- Applying exemplary environmental standards and processes can achieve higher short-term performance, while creating value for the society in the long-run.

FINANCIAL

VALUE

CREATION

=

RETURN

SPREAD

CREATING AND MAXIMIZING FINANCIAL VALUE
THE FINANCIAL VALUE CREATION CYCLE

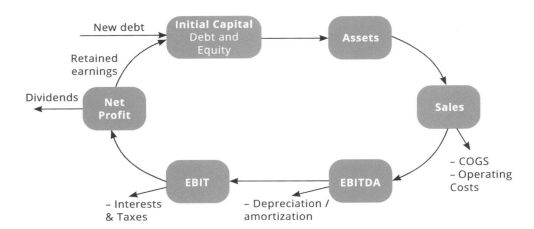

To create value, a company invests capital (equity + debt) in assets, which will, in turn, generate sales:

- Equity is owned money, e.g. owners' private money.
- Debt is loaned money, e.g. a bank loan.
- Assets are resources with an economic value. They can be:
  — Physical (or tangible): cash, equipment, buildings, etc.
  — Non-physical: financial assets (shares, bonds, etc.), intangible assets (software, leases, patents, trademarks, copyrights, etc.).

To generate those sales, it will need to pay for the **Cost of Goods Sold** (COGS, e.g. raw materials) and **operating costs** (e.g. salaries, marketing, etc.).

It will also factor-in the wear of assets (**depreciation and amortization[1]**).

Subtracting these costs, the company gets the Earnings Before Interests and Taxes (EBIT), which is a key financial metric. It represents the value generated by the company, that will be claimed by debt holders, tax authorities and shareholders.

Once the company has made debt and corporate taxes payments, it holds a **net profit or loss (also called earnings after tax or net income).** This profit or loss impacts the company value.

If positive, net profit can be either distributed to shareholders through **dividends,** or **reinvested** in the business (**retained earnings**).

Retained earnings will allow to seek more debt to invest in assets and to **start a new cycle with more assets,** hopefully more sales, and more profit.

1. An asset purchase leads to a cash outflow, but only a fraction of that sum is recorded every year in the P&L, to account for the fact that it will be used over many years. E.g. a car purchased may be depreciated over 5 years. 20% of the cost would then be deducted each year. Depreciation rates are set by tax agencies.

FINANCIAL STATEMENTS

Three key financial statements must be produced by companies on a regular basis to enable informed decision-making (for the management and shareholders):

- The **income statement** (or P&L): this is the **most important statement for business strategy** as it is a good **indicator of the profitability** of a business.
- The **balance sheet**: it is less used by consultants but conceptually important. It also reflects some key corporate strategy choices (e.g. the financial structure).
- The **cash flow statement**: it is important to understand the day-to-day viability of a company. It is also **used for project or company valuation**.
  We will park this one for now and review it in more details in the Valuation chapter (page 120).

---

1 **INCOME STATEMENT (P&L: PROFIT & LOSS)**	2 **BALANCE SHEET**	3 **CASH FLOW STATEMENT**
Captures the revenue and expenses of the company over a period of a time.	Summarizes the assets, liabilities and shareholders' equity at a given time.	Documents the money flowing in and out of the company over a period of time.
	Liabilities are all the sources of funding allowing to fund the company assets.	

ASSETS = LIABILITIES + OWNERS' EQUITY

SIMPLIFIED PROFIT & LOSS (P&L)

Company A
Profit & Loss Statement (P&L)
1st January year n – 31st December year n+1

	Gross Sales	Gross income generated by the company's activity.
–	**Deductions**	Sales allowances, sales discounts, sales returns.
=	Net Sales	Net income generated by the company's activity.
–	**COGS**	Cost Of Goods Sold (variable costs, e.g. raw materials)
=	Gross Profit	
–	**Operating Costs**	Operating (fixed) costs e.g. rent, R&D, marketing.
=	EBITDA	Earning Before Interests, Taxes, Depreciation and Amortization.
–	**Depreciation**	
–	**Amortization**	
=	EBIT or Operating Profit	Earning Before Interest and Taxes.
–	**Financial Costs and Taxes**	
=	Net Income	

SIMPLIFIED BALANCE SHEET

Company A
Balance Sheet
31st December year n+1

CURRENT ASSETS	LIABILITIES
+ Cash & cash equivalents	+ Short-term debt
+ Accounts receivables	+ Account payables
+ Inventories	+ Accrued Expenses
+ Prepaid expenses	+ Long-term liabilities
	= TOTAL LIABILITIES

FIXED ASSETS	
+ Tangible assets	SHAREHOLDERS' EQUITY
+ Intangible assets	+ Shareholders' equity
= TOTAL ASSETS	= TOTAL LIABILITIES + SHAREHOLDERS' EQUITY

CURRENT ASSETS INCLUDE:

- Cash and cash equivalents, i.e. investments with maturity below 1 year
- Accounts receivables, i.e. what clients owe to the firm
- Inventories, i.e. raw materials, work-in-progress, and finished goods
- Prepaid expenses, i.e. payment for a service or good consumed after the balance sheet reporting date.

FIXED ASSETS INCLUDE:

- Tangible assets, e.g. plants, machinery, etc.
- Intangible assets, e.g. patents, copyrights, goodwill, etc.

CURRENT LIABILITIES INCLUDE:

- Short-term debt, e.g. bank overdraft
- Accounts payables, i.e. what the company owes to suppliers
- Accrued expenses, i.e. payments due but not done yet, e.g. accrued leave entitlements.
- Long-term liabilities, e.g. long-term debt or long-term incentives.

Shareholders' equity includes reinvested earnings.

COMPANY VALUE-ADD

WACC

Investors bringing equity expect a certain return on that investment, proportionate to the level of risk involved.

Similarly, the company can decide to **borrow debt with different time horizons**. Long-term debt tends to be more expensive (high interest rate) than medium-term and short-term debt.

In simple terms, the **Weighted Average Cost of Capital (WACC) averages out the equity return and debt interest rates.**

$$\text{WACC} = \underbrace{\frac{E}{V} \times R_e}_{\text{Capital component}} + \underbrace{\frac{D}{V} \times R_d \times (1 - T_c)}_{\text{Debt component}}$$

With:

- R_e = Equity return[2]
- R_d = Debt interest rate
- E = Market value of the firm's equity
- D = Market value of the firm's debt
- V = E+D = Total market value of the firm's financing (equity + debt)
- T_c = Corporate tax rate.

2. Equity return = Dividends per share (for next year)/current market value of stock + growth rate of dividends.

ROCE

In the mid-to-long term, the company will be able to generate a Return On Capital Employed[3] (ROCE):

$$\text{ROCE} = \frac{\text{EBIT}}{\text{Capital Employed}} = \underbrace{\frac{\text{Sales}}{\text{Capital Employed}}}_{\text{Asset turnover}} \times \underbrace{\frac{\text{EBIT}}{\text{Sales}}}_{\text{Operating Margin}}$$

3. Capital Employed = assets – current liabilities (i.e. short-term debt, accounts payables, accrued expenses) = equity + non-current liabilities (mid-to-long-term debt and obligations).

RETURN SPREAD

The Return Spread indicates whether the company creates value:

$$\text{Return Spread} = \text{ROCE} - \text{WACC}$$

- If the **return spread is above 1**, the company **creates value**.
- If the **return spread is below 1**, the company **destroys value**.

MAXIMIZING INVESTOR VALUE

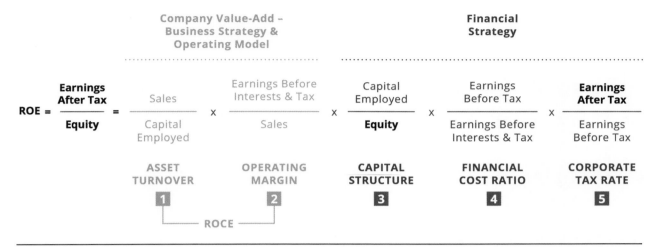

For investors, maximizing value most often means optimizing the earnings (after tax) generated for a given level of equity invested initially. The corresponding financial ratio is the **Return on Equity (ROE).** ROE helps investors compare the company profitability vs. similar players in an industry.

This ROE can be broken down into five key components.
The first two reflect the **business strategy and operating model:**

1 **ASSET TURNOVER**	Reflects the sales generation potential of the assets.
2 **OPERATING MARGIN**	Reflects the efficiency of the operating model i.e. are we delivering the offer in the most efficient way, with the lowest possible costs?

The next three reflect the **financial strategy**:

3 **CAPITAL STRUCTURE**	Reflects the relative importance of equity vs. non-current liabilities, e.g. mid-to-long term debt, long-term obligations.
4 **FINANCIAL COST RATIO**	Reflects the cost of debt. The more expensive the debt, the lower the Earnings Before Tax.
5 **CORPORATE TAX RATE**	Function of the geographic footprint and legal structure of the company, e.g. parent holding with subsidiaries, etc.

In the next chapters, we will look at:
- **Business Strategy**, which aims at **optimizing the first 2 components of this ROE (i.e the ROCE)** in a defined market and ecosystem.
- **Corporate Strategy**, which will look at the **organization more broadly, including the financial strategy** choices (financial structure, cost of debt, footprint and corporate tax).

WHICH "STRATEGY"?

"Strategy" encompasses multiple realities, depending on the stakeholders and scope considered. It is thus helpful to have a sense of the level at which we operate when we define a strategy, as goals, performance indicators, strategic levers and options on the table need to suit that level.

For instance, we could conceptually look at 4 levels:

1 COUNTRY/STATE

Each government pursues a mix of **short and long term economic** (e.g. GDP growth, public debt reduction) **and social** (e.g. health, education, security, freedom...) **value** increase for its citizens. It makes as a result strategic investment choices across the **portfolio of sectors and ecosystems**, leveraging national assets and value-creating organizations. Its playing field can be national, regional, global.

2 CORPORATE/ MULTI-SECTOR

Corporate organizations or conglomerates aim to **maximize value for shareholders**. Companies define their **ownership and financial strategy**, as well as their investment tradeoffs across a **portfolio of Strategic Business Segments/ Business Units** (BUs). They also optimize their **footprint and organizational structure** across markets.

3 SECTOR/ INDUSTRY/ CLUSTER ECOSYSTEM

Public and private stakeholders can **shape or influence a whole economic sector or ecosystem**. An ecosystem comprises **interconnected organizations and individuals competing or partnering to deliver value propositions** to customers. Most, if not all, ecosystems are in some way regulated. Ecosystems can remain very stable or on the contrary undergo significant evolutions or disruptions. Ecosystems can sometimes be geographically grouped in an "economic cluster", to accelerate synergies and partnerships and maximize economic and social value creation (e.g. the Silicon Valley or Hollywood).

4 BUSINESS-UNIT/ SINGLE-SECTOR COMPANY

BUs operate in a defined market and aim to **deliver compelling value propositions** to **target customers** and **win market share**. To do this **profitably**, they need to define their role in the value chain and put together a cost-effective operating model. They do this **over time** taking into account higher-level factors (trends, regulators and governments).

Keep in mind this highest-to-lowest level hierarchy and the types of choices at the different levels. It will be **very important** when we learn how **to solve case studies**.

In the following chapters, **we will focus first on the lowest levels of this hierarchy (4 and 3)**, to make sure you have a good grasp of the fundamental ecosystem dynamics, **before layering-up a corporate strategy lens (2)**.

If you master these, you should be able to easily apply the **same principles** to a **country/state strategy** as we can easily draw a **parallel with corporate strategy**: it aims to manage and optimize for the full **portfolio of sectors** (with different goals and constraints) in that territory.

CHAPTER 5
BUSINESS-UNIT STRATEGY
FUNDAMENTAL ECOSYSTEM DYNAMICS AND BUSINESS STRATEGY CONCEPTS

We saw previously that the Return on Equity can be broken down into 5 components.

Business-Unit (BU) strategy focuses on the first 2 components: the **asset turnover** and **operating margin**.

Note that multiplying these two components gives the ROCE (EBIT/Capital Employed), which is the main **driver of value creation (Return Spread = ROCE – WACC).**

The most **fundamental BU equation** is:

> **PROFIT (BOTTOM LINE) = SALES (TOP LINE) – COSTS**

A BU strategy essentially aims at:

- **Growing** the business (increasing sales i.e. the **"TOP LINE"**)...
- **Profitably** (keeping profit margin or costs as a % of sales reasonable), so that the profit grows in absolute terms (the **"BOTTOM LINE"**), and...
- **Sustainably over time**.

Note: in financial and practical terms, the – overly simplistic – equation above is often written as:

> **EBITDA = NET SALES – COGS – OPERATING EXPENSES**
>
> or
>
> **EBIT = NET SALES – COGS – OPERATING EXPENSES – DEPRECIATION/AMORTIZATION**

PROFIT

=

SALES

−

COSTS

HOW TO PROFITABLY GROW?
A. WHERE CAN WE GROW?

The first step to define a growth strategy is to shortlist the growth opportunities on the table, before diving into a more comprehensive assessment of the possible ways to seize them.

Let's list strategic growth options, from the smallest to the largest scale.

1 GROW CURRENT MARKET/OFFER

Assuming you have a current offering in a market, you can decide to focus on optimizing revenue for that offering. You will thus try to optimize customer number and revenue per customer, noting that these two components are interdependent.

2 EXTEND REACH OF CURRENT OFFERING OR INTRODUCE ADJACENT OFFERING

One step further, you can decide to expand your offering and/or reach to drive more revenue combining: new geographies, customer segments and value propositions (including channels).

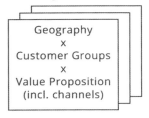

3 EXPAND ROLE ON THE VALUE CHAIN

You could also decide to expand up or down the value chain, taking on the roles of your suppliers or of your direct clients (e.g. distributors), and capturing more value.

4 ENTER A SIGNIFICANTLY DIFFERENT MARKET

You can also decide to broaden the definition of your target market and as a result focus on new customers and customer needs, and possibly a different value chain and ecosystem.

B. HOW TO PRACTICALLY EXECUTE/IMPLEMENT?

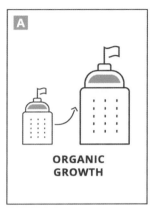

ORGANIC GROWTH

MERGER & ACQUISITION (M&A)

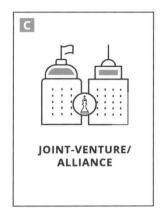

JOINT-VENTURE/ ALLIANCE

Let's assume we have shortlisted a few growth opportunities. Pursuing these would have implications on the operating model, impacting the profit margin and as a result the EBIT(DA). There may be also corporate risks associated.

Ultimately, we may have the flexibility to **pursue a growth opportunity on our own – organic growth –** or prefer or need to do a **merger or acquisition – M&A –**, or set-up a **strategic alliance, e.g. a joint venture – JV**.

To decide between these options, we need to **consider**:

- **The role(s) on the value chain and the level of service needed:**
  — To deliver the value proposition.
  — To communicate the value proposition.
  — To make the value proposition accessible.

- The **capabilities and scale** required to deliver that level of service.
- The **financial, risk and speed impacts** of building these capabilities ourselves vs. "leapfrogging" with inorganic growth, noting that:
  — Mergers and acquisitions may be limited by antitrust laws; they may as well induce significant purchase and integration costs.
  — Alliances mean sharing the intellectual property and the value generated.

- The likely **competitive response.**

ECOSYSTEM DYNAMICS
THE ECOSYSTEM MAP

Listing strategic growth options is a great start, but to assess them, you will often need to understand the market dynamics involved.

We propose here the "Ecosystem Map", a visual framework to help you remember how stakeholders interact and influence each other, in a logical way.

ECOSYSTEM MAP[1]

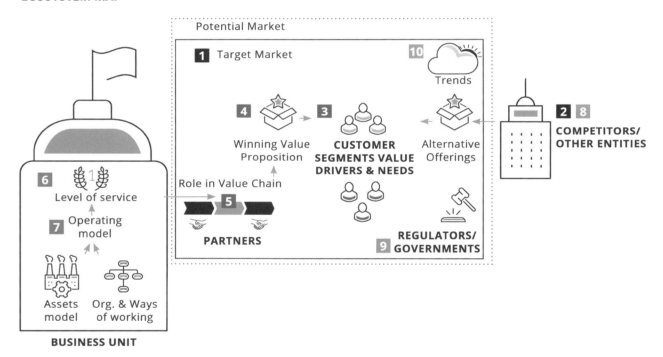

1. The Ecosystem Map covers more or less the same components as Michael Porter's "Five Forces" framework, but it organizes and sequences them to illustrate the interdependencies between stakeholders and components.

MARKET DEFINITION & STRUCTURE

1 The **target market** sets the frame of the analysis.

2 The **market structure** significantly influences the ecosystem.

TOP LINE

3 **Customers** have value drivers and unmet needs.

4 A BU strives to make a **winning value proposition** vs. alternative offerings.

5 The BU top line results from the success of the value proposition and the **role(s) in the value chain** (and profit model).

BOTTOM LINE

6 The BU sets the **level of service** required to fulfill the role(s).

7 The BU implements an **operating model** to deliver this level of service, aiming to maximize its return on assets.

ECOSYSTEM DYNAMICS

8 **Competitors** also make strategic moves or respond to the BU strategy.

9 **Regulators and governments** shape and influence the ecosystem.

10 Short and long-term **trends** impact or disrupt the ecosystem stakeholders.

We will detail each of these components in the following pages.

MARKET DEFINITION AND STRUCTURE
TARGET ADDRESSABLE MARKET

COMPANIES NEED TO DEFINE THEIR TARGET MARKET TO KEEP THE STRATEGY AND OPERATIONS MANAGEABLE, AND FOCUS THEIR EFFORT.

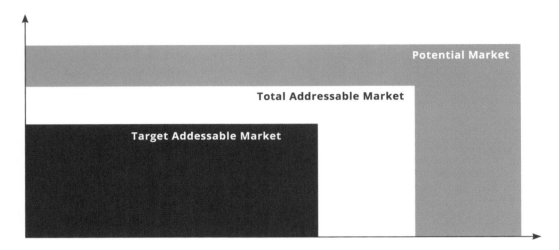

We usually make the distinction between:

- The **potential market**: encompassing anyone potentially interested in the company value offering(s).
- The **total addressable market**: the portion of the potential market that is accessible considering the company capabilities.
- The **target addressable market**: the portion of the addressable market where the company aims to take a strong competitive position.

As a classic example, Coca-Cola can decide whether their target market is:

- Refreshments (competing with a broad range of products)
- Refreshing drinks (competing with water, beers, cold juices etc.)
- Sodas (competing with Schweppes, Pepsi, Fanta etc.)
- Colas (competing with Pepsi, local colas etc.).

MARKET STRUCTURE

Within a target market, companies usually aim to capture volume and value market share. The market structure describes the level of fragmentation of this market share and often reflects the level of maturity of the industry/technology.

The market structure can be more or less dynamic. High growth industries usually attract new competitors (new entrants). Their ability to succeed is highly dependent on the number of industry barriers (e.g. you cannot become a telecom operator without an access to an infrastructure network and a government license).

CONCENTRATED MARKET

Markets where 2 or 3 players capture the vast majority of the market are called concentrated.

Example: the computer or mobile operating systems market.

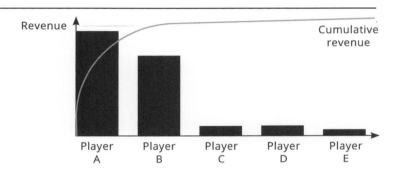

HIGHLY COMPETITIVE MARKET

Markets with 4-5 competitors, each owning 15-25% of the market, are usually highly competitive as each player aims to become the leader.

Example: big 4 services firms.

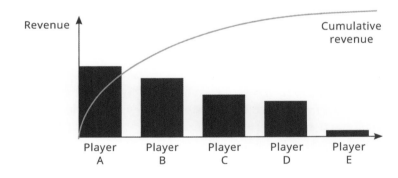

FRAGMENTED MARKET

Markets with a large number of players are called fragmented and are usually seen in immature markets. They usually evolve towards concentration as some players disappear and others consolidate (bankruptcies, alliances, M&A, etc.).

Example: cryptocurrencies.

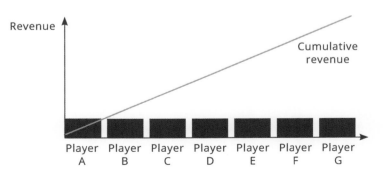

TOP LINE
CUSTOMER NEEDS AND OPPORTUNITIES

COMPANIES STRIVE TO UNDERSTAND CUSTOMER NEEDS TO IDENTIFY BUSINESS OPPORTUNITIES WITHIN THEIR TARGET MARKET.

CUSTOMER JOURNEY

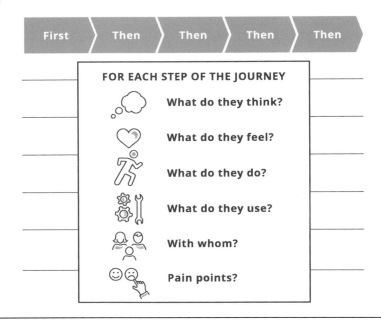

While in the past products or services have been the primary focus of companies, nowadays the **starting point really is the customers and their needs**.

Within a defined target market, companies conduct research to understand **who their (potential) customers are, what their known and unknown desires and pain points are, in their daily life or when they consume the product or service**.

To systematically gather this information, **it is now standard to put together a "customer journey". This allows to list growth or efficiency opportunities**.

BUYING PROCESS

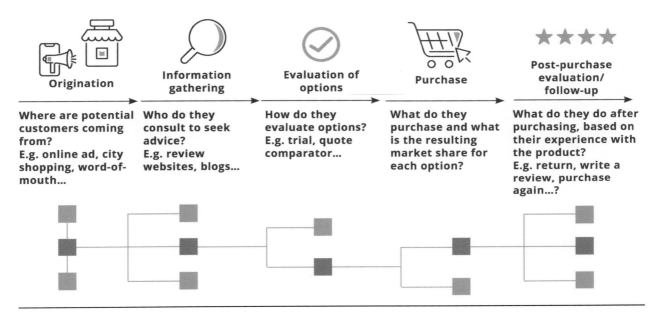

Origination	Information gathering	Evaluation of options	Purchase	Post-purchase evaluation/ follow-up
Where are potential customers coming from? E.g. online ad, city shopping, word-of-mouth…	Who do they consult to seek advice? E.g. review websites, blogs…	How do they evaluate options? E.g. trial, quote comparator…	What do they purchase and what is the resulting market share for each option?	What do they do after purchasing, based on their experience with the product? E.g. return, write a review, purchase again…?

An alternative approach (less customer-centric but helpful still), called a **buying process,** consists in mapping out the **sequence of decisions** leading to a purchase in the current target market, **and for each decision, the possible outcomes.**

This leads to a **decision tree** which can be used qualitatively or can be quantified in a very thorough manner.

Once built at the desired granularity level with market research and analytics, companies can select the decision points and outcomes they want to shift.

Note that the buying process does not capture the factors driving one or another outcome.

Regardless of the framework(s) used to identify opportunities, the next step is to prioritize the ones to pursue. In a case study, it will thus be key to have crystal clear clarity on the business or project objectives and decision-making criteria, to assess and logically prioritize opportunities identified.

TOP LINE
TARGET CUSTOMER SEGMENTS

CUSTOMERS ARE SEGMENTED AND PRIORITIZED, BASED ON THEIR DISTINCT FEATURES, BEHAVIORS, AND BUSINESS POTENTIAL RELATIVE TO THE BUSINESS OPPORTUNITY.

CUSTOMER SEGMENTATION FRAME

Illustrative

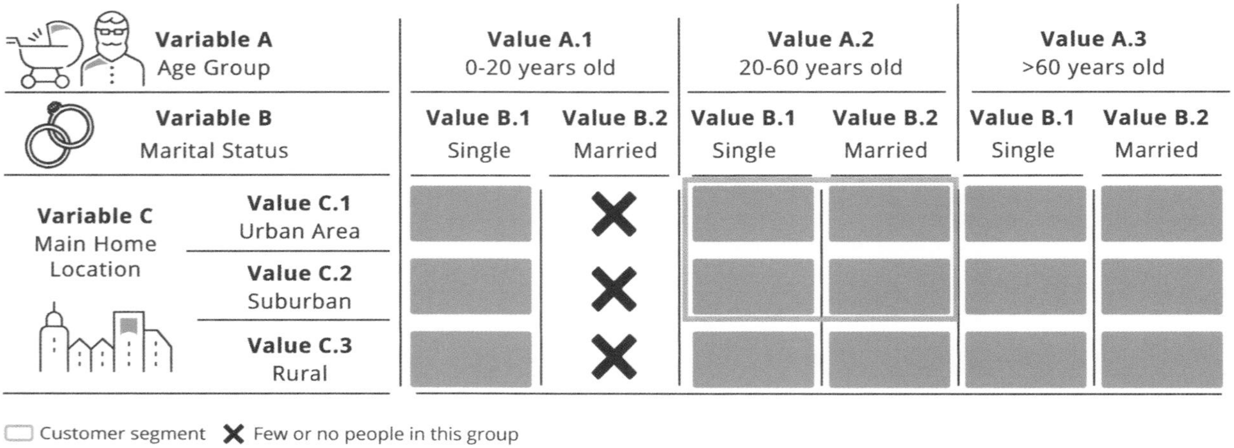

		Value A.1 0-20 years old		Value A.2 20-60 years old		Value A.3 >60 years old	
Variable A Age Group		Value B.1 Single	Value B.2 Married	Value B.1 Single	Value B.2 Married	Value B.1 Single	Value B.2 Married
Variable B Marital Status							
Variable C Main Home Location	**Value C.1** Urban Area	�	✗	▬	▬	▬	▬
	Value C.2 Suburban	▬	✗	▬	▬	▬	▬
	Value C.3 Rural	▬	✗	▬	▬	▬	▬

▭ Customer segment   ✗ Few or no people in this group

Prioritized opportunities will usually have several potential customer groups, each with different profiles and behaviors.

Customer behaviors (e.g. purchasing a product or recommending it to friends) are driven by many contextual factors, which often cannot be influenced (e.g. individuals' cultural background in B2C, or company historical way of doing things in B2B context, etc.).

Behaviors can also be correlated with customer attributes (e.g. demographics for B2C, company characteristics for B2B).

Customer segmentation aims at breaking down customers into sufficiently distinct clusters, allowing to predict their attitudes, preferences and potential while keeping complexity manageable (few BUs can efficiently manage more than 4 or 5 client segments).

The main challenge is to identify the different customer variables (and values for each) that will lead to distinct segments with meaningfully different behaviors and value drivers.

For instance, if Nvidia or AMD launched a brand new – but incredibly expensive – quantum graphics card, should they primarily target:

- Computer companies e.g. Apple, Toshiba, etc. (as an OEM)?
- The defence industry?
- Professionals in the TV/Cinema industry?
- Gamers?

Once consistent segments are identified, it is possible to conduct a prioritization exercise to define target segments, and allocate a share of the go-to-market investment.

In a case study, you should **align on the assessment criteria with the interviewer**.

If the interviewer asks you for a framework, you may want to cross **attractiveness and feasibility** or consider using the slightly more methodical framework outlined below.

Regardless of the criteria used, it is often meaningful to prioritize segments over time, e.g. "Low hanging fruit", "mid-term opportunity", etc.

CUSTOMER SEGMENTS PRIORITIZATION EXAMPLE FRAMEWORK

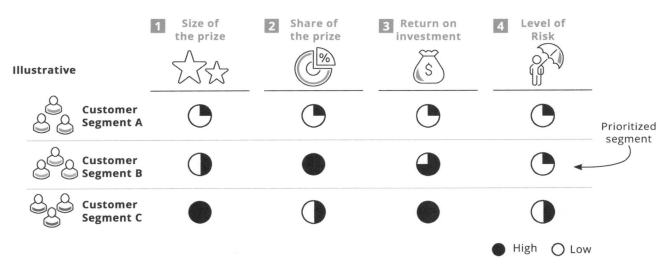

1 What is the maximum **SIZE OF THE PRIZE**, considering:

- The potential customer base
- Their estimated willingness to pay?

2 What is our plausible **SHARE OF THE PRIZE**, considering:

- Our current share in the market
- The competitive intensity
- The ability of the market to hear about, access and adopt our offer?

3 What is the expected **RETURN ON INVESTMENT**, considering:

- The upfront and running costs to create/seize the opportunity
- The sustainability of the opportunity (expected growth/decline/cycles)
- The market share sustainability (barriers to entry)?

4 Companies can also balance the financial opportunity with the **LEVEL OF RISK**, e.g.:

- Level of fixed (and potentially sunk) costs in case of failure
- Corporate risk(s) associated with the opportunity (e.g. legal, compliance)
- Level of cultural change required.

TOP LINE
VALUE PROPOSITION

A VALUE PROPOSITION IS AN OFFER MADE TO CUSTOMERS, IN EXCHANGE FOR SOMETHING.

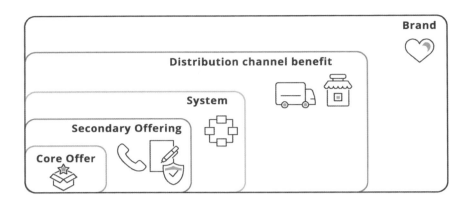

While in the past "offer" meant "product", it is now taken in its broadest sense.

The offer can encompass:

- At a minimum the **core offer** i.e. a physical product, a digital asset (e.g. a bitcoin), a service or a right granted (e.g. temporary license).
- A **secondary offering** that directly enhances the core offer (e.g. a customer service or a long-term guarantee).
- **A system** around the core offer, that extends its usage or amplifies its benefits (e.g. Microsoft Office 365 suite).
- **Distribution channel benefit**, such as channel interoperability (e.g. my order history is visible to customer service in all channels), or unique channel experience (e.g. dedicated space for customers to work in a car servicing center).
- The company or product **brand and the perceptions and beliefs** it projects (luxury, quality, environmentally friendly...).

Customers accepting the offer can provide in return:

- A **financial asset** (e.g. money, option...).
- **Information** (e.g. data on their personal life and networks to Facebook, their professional network to LinkedIn).
- **Rights** (e.g. by leaving money on a savings account, they give the bank the right to invest it).
- **Time and effort** (e.g. neighbors bartering services).

ALTERNATIVE OFFERINGS

CUSTOMERS WITH A NEED CHOOSE – CONSCIOUSLY OR NOT – BETWEEN SEVERAL ALTERNATIVE OFFERS, EACH WITH A SPECIFIC VALUE PROPOSITION.

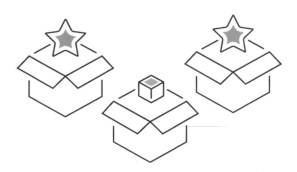

From the company perspective, these alternative offers are usually divided in two groups:

1 Directly competing offerings (competitors): these aim to meet customer needs in a similar way as the company, sharing many offer attributes.

- Netflix is for instance directly competing with TV channels VOD services.

2 Substitutes are different offers fulfilling the same customer functional needs or value drivers.

- On-demand movies could for instance be seen as a substitute for movie theatres as both give the opportunity to customers to watch an entertaining program.

Note the breadth of competing offerings and substitutes is directly derived by how the company defines its target market.

- E.g. for the Coca-Cola example we mentioned earlier, are we competing in the soda, beverages or refreshments market?

TOP LINE
WINNING VALUE PROPOSITION
TO BE ADOPTED AND SUCCESSFUL, THE VALUE PROPOSITION MUST BE COMPELLING, COMMUNICATED AND ACCESSIBLE FOR TARGET SEGMENTS

---

1 COMPELLING

Companies build compelling value propositions for their target customer segments by:

- First identifying **customer needs and value drivers**
- Then **tailoring the offer** attributes to **meet those functional and emotional needs**.

This can be articulated using a **benefit ladder**, a marketing framework introduced in the 1980s by Philip Kotler and Kevin Lane Keller and still used today (see illustration on next page).

Attributes – at the bottom of the ladder – drive the **functional and emotional benefits**. Attributes are not valuable per se. They are the "reasons to believe" the functional and emotional benefits.

Attributes that do not help meet the target customers' functional or emotional needs are unnecessary and can be removed from the offer.

To be differentiated, **companies conduct a similar exercise for competitors** to make sure benefit ladders/value propositions are different enough to be clearly distinguished by target customers.

Claims should be **valid for a long-enough period** as it is counter-productive to change frequently the value proposition and claims.

BENEFIT LADDER
Illustration - Smarphone A

		User Segment 1 Teenagers	User Segment 2 Young parents	User Segment 3 Mid-50s
Emotional Benefits		Feel integrated within the rest of the teenager community	Joy of sharing how their kids are growing	Feel young and connected, in control of the modern tech
Functional Benefits		Allows to stream VOD anywhere	High quality camera	User-friendly interface
Attributes		14 cm high, 7 cm wide, 180g, processor X, operating system OSA, touch screen, wifi, bluetooth, 5G, 240 go storage.		

2 COMMUNICATED

Once the benefit ladder is clearly articulated, the value proposition can be turned into **messages,** emphasizing the unique and compelling functional and emotional benefits, as well as the key supporting attributes (the "reason to believe").

To communicate these messages to target customers, companies need to have a good understanding of the **customers' profiles** (e.g. habits, sources of information, trusted advisors, devices and channels used, etc.).

This allows to define an efficient **omnichannel customer engagement model** – e.g. with channels talking to each other, push/pull interactions, etc. –, via which (multichannel) **marketing campaigns** can be delivered and customer needs addressed**.**

3 ACCESSIBLE

This understanding also helps define the most efficient **distribution channels** (e.g. in retail stores, online only, combination, direct or through wholesalers and retailers etc.), which is key to make the offer **accessible** to target customers **at a manageable cost**.

Last but not least, the company must set-up its **operations** (including supply chain) to make sure this accessibility is **reliable** (no shortages or capacity issue).

TOP LINE

ROLE IN THE VALUE CHAIN

COMPANIES DEFINE THE ROLE THEY WANT TO PLAY IN THE VALUE CHAIN TO DELIVER THIS WINNING VALUE PROPOSITION TO TARGET CUSTOMERS

VALUE CHAIN

Illustration – Vertical Integration

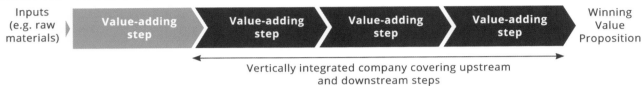

VALUE CHAIN

The value chain is a framework to represent (usually with chevrons) the **key steps required to turn an idea or raw products into an end offer** delivered to customers.

It is usually described at the ecosystem level (e.g. food crop > production > harvesting > primary processing > secondary processing > packaging > wholesale and retail).

Value chains can also be mapped at the firm level, with key operational processes contributing to the firm value chain (see Key Activities & Level of Service page 88).

PRORITIZING ROLES

A company willing to bring a value proposition to market will evaluate **for each role** its **ability to be more competitive** than others:

- Can we meet customers' needs more effectively than other companies?
- For the same output, are we more efficient (cost-effective) than other companies?

The company will also evaluate the **level of risk** of certain roles and decide whether it matches the management's appetite for risk.

Having finite resources, the company can then **decide to focus on one or several roles**.

Illustration B – Specialization

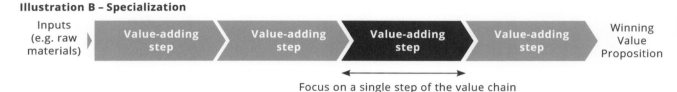

Focus on a single step of the value chain
(e.g. packaging)

Companies can, for instance, **make the strategic choice to be focused on a single step** in the value chain, **or to cover upstream and downstream steps ("vertically integrated"** companies).

There is no right or wrong answer there. Key considerations include:

- **Vertical integration** can allow to:
  — Get a **higher share of the value** by capturing the incremental margin at each step.
  — **Secure inputs** or making it harder for competitors to access them.
  — Maintain **quality** standards throughout the steps.
  — Provide the **scale** required **to compete in oligopoly markets** (e.g. mobile phone providers).

- **Specialization**, focusing on a single step of the value chain may:
  — Allow to **focus investments** on a specific type of assets and **reach a competitive advantage** (cost reduction or product differentiation).
  — Give more **flexibility** to refocus activities should customer needs evolve.

TOP LINE
SUPPLIERS, PARTNERS AND PROFIT MODEL

PARTNERING

Companies need to establish partnerships with other organizations to be able to deliver the customer value proposition (for roles not fulfilled in the value chain, e.g. suppliers).

These can be **formal** (binding parties with a contract for mutual benefits, e.g. lower price for party A, volume predictability for party B) or **informal**, depending on the degree of flexibility and quality consistency required.

PROFIT MODEL

The company must define (and agree with its partners) its profit model as part of the value chain.

Profit models are defined by two dimensions:

1. **How to monetize the role to partners downstream in the value chain e.g.:**
   — Direct margin (price markup) on product being developed or distributed
   — Fee for service (set fee, fee for usage, loan interest, share of profit generated)
   — Monetize rights for commercial use (intellectual property licensing, franchise)
   — Monetize access to customers and to their data (e.g. Google Adwords, Facebook).

2. **The time horizon for the payment:**
   — One-off purchase
   — Long-term engagement/recurring payment (e.g. buying a low-cost printer actually binds the customer to buy expensive ink cartridges later on).

Note: a company profit model is not necessarily directly monetizing the core offer but can be a by-product (Google offers you a great search engine and other services but makes money by selling ads and services based on your details to other firms).

NEGOTIATION – "BARGAINING" – POWER

Negotiations are required to agree on the value provided and captured by each stakeholder along the value chain.

In most transactions, **one company will have a stronger negotiation or bargaining power** than the other(s). This power gives the ability to obtain better terms and to capture more profit for the service provided.

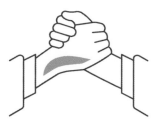

Drivers of the bargaining power are the:

- **Relative business importance**:
  - Concentration of supplier's supplies in client purchases — if I offer a preferred procurement model to a supplier, I may be able to negotiate discounts.
  - Importance of client's purchases in supplier's sales — if I am one of the largest customers of my supplier, I may negotiate discounts.

- **Substitutability**, function of the:
  - Concentration of suppliers — if I have no choice for suppliers, I am in a weaker position.
  - Level of differentiation — not all suppliers provide the same value proposition.
  - Transfer costs — current systems or processes might be optimized to operate with one supplier, and changing suppliers might incur costs or issues.
  - Level of transparency on respective margins.
  - The ease of integrating vertically to replace the supplier.

SECURING AFFORDABLE SUPPLIES

Some industries rely on rare resources (e.g. raw materials or expertise).

Part of a business **strategy includes securing long-term access to those key resources**, and potentially aiming to reduce competitors' access to them.

Companies can do this by:

- Integrating vertically (upstream)
- Establishing long-term contracts – e.g. commodity futures – to:
  - Guarantee volume and/or price
  - Mitigate currency fluctuation risk.

TOP LINE – PRICING DEEP-DIVE
WHICH PRICING METHOD SHOULD YOU USE?

PRICING ALGORITHM

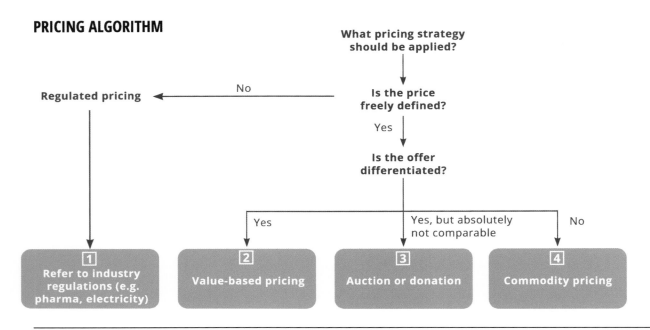

When the value proposition includes a fee to be paid by the customer, a price needs to be defined. Key considerations include (in this order):

1 Are prices freely defined (free pricing) in this industry/geography or are they regulated (e.g. pharmaceutical products, energy)?

If they are **regulated**, you need to deep-dive to **understand the pricing mechanisms:** which constraints apply? How is the price set?

2 Is it possible to **compare and differentiate** the product with another company product, even slightly? If so, **value-based pricing** should apply (see next page).

3 If elements **cannot be referenced** or quantified (e.g. price for an unique or impossible experience), use an **auction** – ensuring costs are covered – to maximize profit; if you do not need this revenue stream to run the business, you can also consider **donations**.

4 If the offer is **absolutely not differentiated** among competitors, **commodity pricing** then applies (see page 87).

VALUE-BASED PRICING

Illustrative

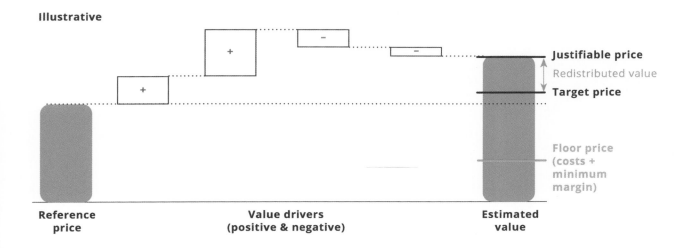

In most business cases involving a pricing question, value-based pricing will apply.

Value-based pricing relies on the idea that a price can to some extent be justified by a breakdown of the value it brings compared to other alternatives.

For that reason, **the value perceived differs from one customer segment to another.** You thus need to evaluate first the perceived value for each customer segment.

To be compelling, it is better to stick to **quantifiable value drivers (economic benefits and costs).** Unquantifiable benefits can be kept as an additional argument when selling the offer.

Practically, for a given customer segment, we usually **take as a reference the leading competing alternative offering in the category** and look at the benefits and costs associated with it, compared to our solution, to get to a justifiable price:

> **JUSTIFIABLE PRICE FOR OUR OFFER = LEADING COMPETITOR REFERENCE PRICE + ECONOMIC BENEFITS OF OUR OFFER – ECONOMIC COSTS OF OUR OFFER**

To set your target justifiable price:

1. **Calculate your fixed costs** (incl. R&D) **and variable costs** to define a minimum (**floor**) price that guarantees you to break even and provide a minimum and sustainable profit.
2. Calculate your **justifiable price** with the relevant reference competitors and value drivers (positive and negative).
3. Assuming your justifiable price is higher than the competitive reference price, **consider redistributing part of the incremental value** to customers, to further strengthen your value proposition. The more value you give back, the more likely you are to gain market share in that segment.

If you deal with multiple customer segments, evaluate different scenarios, e.g. pricing for the most willing to pay segment and planning for low uptake in less willing segments, or pricing for the majority and anticipating very high uptake in the one(s) willing to pay.

Note: when the customer base is large, you can conduct a **price sensitivity** market research to provide more data points and define an optimal price maximizing profit.

TOP LINE – PRICING DEEP-DIVE
PRICE STRUCTURE

Full or disaggregated pricing

Variable

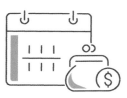

Paid in full or over time
(e.g. subscription)

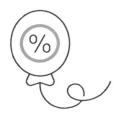

Discount scheme

The **value-based target price** we defined on the previous page is at this stage an **aspirational target price over time**.

The actual price may fluctuate based on different factors (e.g. demand, specials, etc.).

A pricing structure is a practical way to price an offer (i.e. the price showed to the customers) and hopefully achieve the target price. There are hundreds of pricing structures to choose from.

While putting in place sophisticated pricing schemes can theoretically maximize value realized, it can in reality confuse or frustrate the customers.

It can also be associated with a high admin burden, impact cash flow, or lead to a lower average value per customer if poorly designed.

Key dimensions to consider when building a price structure include:

1. Do we propose our offer as a whole with a given price (full price) or do we break down our value offering in different components with different price levels (disaggregated pricing)?
    - E.g. think about the airline low-cost models or the Skype freemium model where a small share of customers pays for the whole network and allow individuals to call for free.

2. Is the price set or variable over time?
    - Airlines use yield management to maximize the value per plane, changing the price of seats over time until the flight departs.

3. Is the price paid in full once (purchase or perpetual license) or is it paid over time (e.g. subscription)?

4. Is a discount scheme in place? If so, is it the same across the customer base or is it differentiated?

COMMODITY PRICING

Illustrative

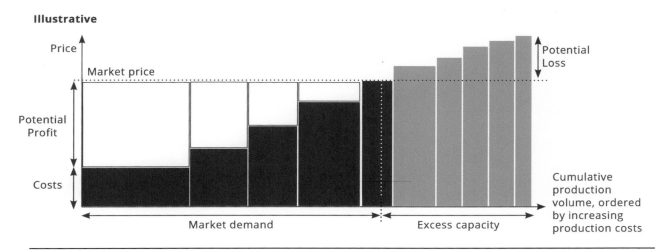

In the rare cases where offerings are fully undifferentiated, customers will choose the least costly. **Price is then set by the marginal cost of production** (the last dark blue producer bar in the chart above).

Tips to read this chart:

- The chart shows the cumulative production, with producers on the X-axis ordered by production costs. The width of each bar represents the producer's production volume. The height of each bar represents the producer's production cost.
- The vertical dotted line indicates the average cumulative market demand volume.
- The horizontal dotted line is the average market price (there can be a lot of fluctuations). It is close to the production cost of the last producer managing to sell its production (the marginal cost producer).
- For each producer, the difference between the average market price and the production cost indicates a potential profit or loss.

- Producers on the left-hand side of the chart are very likely to sell their entire production and make a profit, because they will be able to set a selling price at or slightly below the average market price.
- On the other hand, producers on the right-hand side will struggle to make a profit with their production (unless they can stock it and sell it in the future).

Note: to be representative, the **production costs need to include the full costs**, including for instance transportation and customs taxes.

BOTTOM LINE
KEY ACTIVITIES AND LEVEL OF SERVICE

Illustration – Company Value Chain

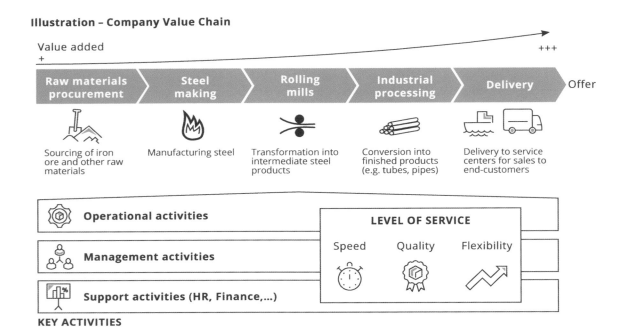

KEY ACTIVITIES

KEY ACTIVITIES/CAPABILITIES

To fulfill its role(s) and meet stakeholders' expectations, the company must deliver a set of:

- **Operational activities** to turn inputs into outputs for customers (e.g. new product development).
- **Management activities** to govern (part of) the organization (e.g. strategy definition, corporate governance).
- **Support activities**, required for the company to operate (e.g. accounting, recruitment...).

While some of these activities are fairly undifferentiated (e.g. payroll), others can play a critical role and are often described as **key business processes or strategic capabilities** (e.g. young talent sourcing for a sports club, procurement for retailers, etc.).

LEVEL OF SERVICE

To operate effectively, the company needs to meet a certain level of service for each key activity (informally or formally defined, e.g. with a Service Level Agreement – SLA).

The "level of service" is a set of constraints on SPEED, QUALITY AND FLEXIBILITY. The higher the level of service, the higher the price charged usually.[2,3]

For instance, a glass company must reliably and consistently produce glass that will be solid enough to not break under standard conditions, with some safety buffer. However, if this glass actually resists to conditions seen once in a century, but is priced like a standard glass, then the company has essentially invested in its offer attributes without communicating the value and charging for it.

2. Management consultants often conduct Business Process Re-engineering (BPR) projects, aiming to streamline processes to improve speed, quality and flexibility.

3. Cost-reduction projects called Zero-Based Budgeting also follow the same principles and list first the core activities to be delivered and the level of service for each, to then quantify the resources to be mobilized for each process and function.

OPERATING MODEL

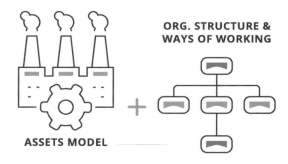

ORG. STRUCTURE & WAYS OF WORKING

ASSETS MODEL

4. A common way to cut down people costs is to reduce the level of people and the cost of people by optimizing "management spans and layers". Management spans describe the number of people managed by a single manager. By setting a minimum number of people reporting into a manager, we can regroup teams and reduce managers. By removing hierarchy layers, we flatten the organization. This allows to remove unnecessary escalation and delegation, and accelerates decision-making processes.

DEFINING THE OPERATING MODEL

There are a million ways to define an "operating model" and as many frameworks to break them down.

We will not claim to have a superior framework, but we will try to guide you with one that we think can help you in strategy interviews.

It should notably help you troubleshoot an operational problem and make recommendations to improve the situation.

If you aim **to ultimately improve the bottom line, the most convincing approach is to optimize the Return on Assets**. This is also a great starting point to quantify the benefits of an operational review.

WE THUS PROPOSE TO DEFINE THE OPERATING MODEL AS THE SUM OF TWO MAJOR COMPONENTS:

1. **ASSETS MODEL: which assets** need to be mobilized to deliver the target level of service, and how are they organized at a high level?
2. **ORGANIZATIONAL STRUCTURE AND WAYS OF WORKING: how to organize and mobilize these assets** in the most effective way?[4]

THE OPERATING MODEL IMPACTS THE ORGANIZATIONAL CULTURE

The culture of the organization is primarily shaped by:

- Its purpose and values
- Its strategy and goals
- Its assets (people, environment and tools)
- Its organizational structure and ways of working
- Its history.

The operating model as defined above thus has a significant impact on the organization culture.

ASSETS MODEL DEEP-DIVE
RETURN ON ASSETS TRADEOFFS

COMPANIES GENERATE VALUE MOBILIZING AND COORDINATING 3 MAJOR TYPES OF ASSETS (OR RESOURCES) TO CONDUCT THEIR OPERATIONAL, MANAGEMENT AND SUPPORT ACTIVITIES

1 PEOPLE

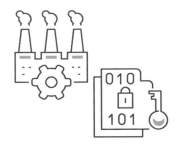

2 TECHNOLOGIES
(hardware & software, patents...)

3 INPUTS
(raw materials, funding, data/information, intellectual property...)

To maximize their Return on Assets (RoA), they need to make **tradeoffs across 3+1 ROA DRIVERS.**

| LEVEL OF ASSETS UTILIZATION | EFFECTIVENESS | COST | + SUSTAINABILITY |

An adequate LEVEL OF ASSETS and UTILIZATION

Too few assets: production will not meet demand.
Too much capacity: unnecessarily high production costs.

Sufficient assets EFFECTIVENESS, to produce high quality outputs at a high rate.

The lowest assets COST possible, for a given level of effectiveness.

+ SUSTAINABLE assets (to delay replacement).

"Right-sizing" organizations or **improving operating performance** requires to **optimize these tradeoffs.** The main challenge is that **these 3+1 drivers are interdependent.** For instance, outsourcing a call center offshore could mean:

More flexibility with on-demand services.

Possibly lower call/service effectiveness (limited training and call quality oversight, language barriers, and time zone mismatch).

Lower cost on average (higher cost per hour but no full time fully loaded salaries).

Risk of outsourcing company bankruptcy/withdrawal.

EXAMPLES OF OPERATING PERFORMANCE METRICS OR QUESTIONS

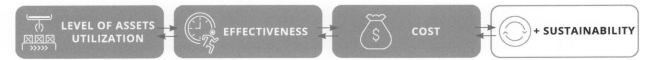

LEVEL OF ASSETS UTILIZATION

- What is the plant uptime (operating time/total scheduled time)?

- What is the consultant's utilization (time fully billed/number of working days)?

- Are we capped in terms of output due to full utilization?

- Do we have flexibility for additional capacity at peak time?

EFFECTIVENESS

- Is this utilization focused on value-creating activities?

- What is the rate to produce outputs?

- What is the quality of outputs (how much is lost/must be re-done)?

COST

- What is the ratio of permanent to casual staff?

- What is the level of overtime?

- How does remuneration compare to benchmarks in each market?

+ SUSTAINABILITY

- What is the employee churn rate?

- Is there a risk of disruption (e.g. rare raw material)?

- Are assets compliant with (future) regulations?

- Is the use of this technology carrying a reputational risk?

ASSETS MODEL DEEP-DIVE
IDEATING ASSETS MODEL OPTIONS

In a case study, you may be asked to recommend changes to the operating model to improve its performance. You can ideate alternative assets model options and list pros and cons along the 3+1 drivers. You will then be able to select a model based on the decision-making criteria, constraints or guiding principles set at the beginning of the case.

You will find below, as a guidance, **6 key questions to diagnose the needs and constraints**, and help you ideate assets model options, once you have clarified the target level of service.

 	Can we meet the target level of service by **AUTOMATING** the activity?	Do we need a **CONSTANT** capacity or do our needs significantly **FLUCTUATE OVER TIME** (during the day, throughout the year, ...)?	Do we have **GEOGRAPHICAL CONSTRAINTS** (logistics, time zones, regulations,....)? Can we have decentralized resources (e.g. as a network)?
Examples			
PEOPLE	Replace customer service with chat bots?	Holiday seasons for the tourism industry	Salesforce needed in field vs. marketing team at HQ/at home
 TECHNOLOGIES	3D-printing vs. manual printing	Dedicated vs. on demand cloud computing capacity	Cement manufacturing plants to be located in customer catchment area due to high delivery constraints and costs
 INPUTS	Automatic web-scraping vs. manual data collection	Steady monthly supply vs. seasonal supply	Export ban on enriched uranium supply accross regions

Note: the alternative **assets model options** you will come up with **will have an implication on the organizational structure**, e.g.:

Super thin core team, operating as a network, and outsourcing all non-core functions to contractors	vs.	Centralized organization with all functions in-house, located in one HQ

Note 2: We purposefully kept choices simple here. In reality, many companies will have to make these asset model choices at the corporate level, factoring-in multiple BUs and/or geographies. Accountability and governance questions then also come into play, complexifying the org. design (see CORPORATE STRATEGY page 108).

 4

Can assets be **IN-HOUSE**? Can they be **RENTED/LICENSED/ OUTSOURCED**? Would any option compromise a competitive advantage (patent...) or increase risk (privacy...)?

▼

Employees vs. contractors or consultants

In-house software vs. Software as a Service (SaaS)

Internally gathered competitive intelligence vs. external competitive intelligence reports

---

 5

Can we meet **QUALITY AND SPEED REQUIREMENTS** with multiple average or low-performing assets (combined) or do we necessarily need highly effective assets?

▼

One global expert vs. a team of local skilled practitioners?

One next-generation machine vs. multiple previous generation machines?

A few experts interviews vs. desktop literature review

 6

For in-house assets, can we envisage a **LESS RIGID OPERATING MODEL** to streamline resourcing?

▼

Can we have talents working for different teams/projects?

Can platforms be tailored for different teams/use cases?

Can we dynamically request and allocate funding throughout the year, instead of traditional annual budgets?

ORG. STRUCTURE AND WAYS OF WORKING

SOME CASE STUDIES REQUIRE TO FOCUS ON INTERNAL FACTORS, NAMELY THE ORGANIZATIONAL STRUCTURE AND THE WAYS OF WORKING

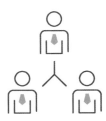

The organizational structure – org. structure – defines **how assets are organized**.
Ways of working encompass the set of **formal or informal systems and principles** that describe **how assets operate** to deliver key activities.

---

1 ORGANIZING PEOPLE AND OTHER ASSETS

- **Team structure (tightly linked to the assets model choices)**, e.g.
  — Functional, center of excellence, agile?
  — Job titles and reporting lines (collectively forming the org chart).
- **Accountabilities, roles and responsibilities**, e.g.
  — Deliverables accountability
  — Decision-making rights.
- **Ownership of/control over other assets** (funding, data, systems, infrastructure, etc.).

2 ORGANIZING THE WORK

- The company must define, **formally** (e.g. with documented cadence and processes) **or informally**: what needs to be done, how is "done" measured, who should do it, and how it should be done.
  The company has "ways of working" for:
  — **Work planning, resource prioritization and allocation**
  — **Work allocation & time management**
  — **Work delivery** (waterfall processes, agile sprints...)
  — **Performance review** (work delivery and progress vs. goals)
  — **Knowledge management** (to replicate work in the future).

Note: a major focus of **Post-Merger Integration** – PMI – projects is to **streamline the organization structure** (to deliver **synergies**) and to **harmonize ways of working.**

3 DRIVING THE RIGHT SKILLS AND BEHAVIOURS

- **HR policies and mechanisms** are put in place to **align skills and behaviors with the strategy and values**, covering for instance:
    - Hiring
    - Incentives and awards (incentivized behaviours are reinforced)
    - Performance tracking and management, feedback, training...
    - Workplace safety, equality, bullying prevention...

- **Leaders and Managers** strongly influence employees' behaviours and performance (positively or negatively), e.g.:
    - Role-modelling: do Leaders & Managers do what they say?
    - Empowerment: are employees encouraged to find the best solution on their own or do they follow instructions?
    - Innovation: is failing accepted and safe?
    - Management focus: do Managers focus on results, on the way the work is done or on presence and effort invested?

- **Team interactions** define how problems are managed and how work is delivered. These include:
    - Collaboration vs. individual culture
    - Communication channels and style
    - Company and team rituals
    - Knowledge management and sharing.

ECOSYSTEM DYNAMICS
COMPETITIVE DYNAMICS

ECOSYSTEMS ARE NOT STATIC. TO BE ROBUST, A BUSINESS STRATEGY NEEDS TO FACTOR IN TRENDS AND COMPETITIVE DYNAMICS.

When defining and stress-testing a Business Strategy, you need to factor in the likely **competitor moves**. Two types of analyses can be conducted:

---

1 MARKET OUTLOOK

What may the next competitor moves be? For instance:

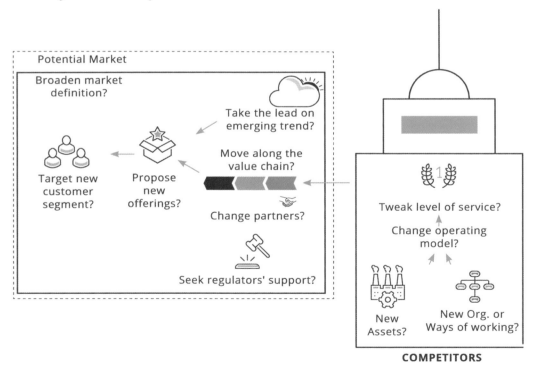

2 COMPETITIVE RESPONSE

What will competitors' response be to your strategy or tactics (e.g. new product)? To do this we usually:

Identify the key **triggering events** that will lead to a competitor response (e.g. everyday low-price announcement).

Evaluate what the competitors' **potential moves** are, following the triggering event:

- Which levers can they pull (e.g. reduce price, threaten shared customers, develop a similar offer, etc.)?
- What could the magnitude of their response be — would they reduce by 5% or halve their prices?

Evaluate the degree of **competitors'** organization **agility or inertia** to respond to our triggering event.

REGULATORS

REGULATORS CAN IMPACT AN ENTIRE ECOSYSTEM:

THE MARKET STRUCTURE AND COMPETITIVE DYNAMICS, E.G.	• Allowing organizations to participate in a market (e.g. safety accreditation). • Preventing dominant market positions (anti-trust). • Preventing uncompetitive tacit or explicit price collusion agreements among companies.
CUSTOMER NEEDS, E.G.	• Forcing customers to consume an offer (e.g. obligation to be immunized). • Forcing companies to provide equal access across the territory (e.g. mobile phone access in some countries).
VALUE OFFERINGS, E.G.	• Controlling and selecting which offers are allowed to be commercialized (e.g. legal vs. illegal drugs). • Regulating price (e.g. for utilities or pharmaceuticals). • Defining the level of Value-Added Tax, impacting the acquisition cost for the end consumer (e.g. food, tobacco, alcohol, petrol).
THE LEVEL OF SERVICE AND THE OPERATING MODEL, E.G.	• People (e.g. equality rules, employment of local resources) • Technologies (e.g. standards to be used – 5G… –, GMO ban, etc.) • Resources (e.g. liquidity coverage ratios for banks, ingredients used for consumer goods, anti-laundering controls on funding). • Processes (e.g. corporate compliance, hygiene, safety and environmental standards, etc.).

For that reason, regulatory strategy in an integral part of a BU strategy and encompasses:
1. **Monitoring**, to understand what the trends and potential changes are.
2. **Stakeholder mapping**, to have clarity on the key decision-makers and influencers.
3. **Lobbying**, to provide a point of view and influence the development of regulations.

GOVERNMENTS & PUBLIC SERVICE

GOVERNMENTS AND PUBLIC ORGANIZATIONS CAN ALSO PLAY AN ACTIVE ROLE, E.G.:

GUARANTEE A PUBLIC SERVICE

E.g. education, consumer health and protection, justice, defense, equity etc.

These are delivered either through:

- Civil servants ("in-house")
- Service provision commissioning/ delegation (e.g. to private companies or to not-for-profit organizations, often via tenders).

5. E.g. economic growth through employment or increased business activity.

FOSTER ONE OR SEVERAL ECOSYSTEMS TO GENERATE SECONDARY ECONOMIC BENEFITS[5]

Options available include:

- Funding public infrastructure.
- Establishing Public-Private Partnerships.
- Providing grants/subsidies/tax incentives to companies and to non-government organizations.

ECOSYSTEM DYNAMICS
TRENDS

TRENDS AND STRATEGY

Strategy outlines the path of the company towards the future. **Understanding the near and long-term future is thus essential to identify plausible scenarios and plan accordingly.**

There is an infinite number of trends, nested under some global megatrends, all impacting this near and long-term future. Think about the **key themes and megatrends** below:

DEMOGRAPHIC SHIFTS, E.G.	• Aging population, immigration, diversity, population growth, suburbanization, etc.
SCIENCE AND TECHNOLOGY, E.G.	• Artifical intelligence, clean energy, bioengineering, digitization, automation, etc. • Pandemics, privacy, ethics, security issues, etc.
ECONOMIC DYNAMICS, E.G.	• Globalization, energy supply, customer experience, individualization, etc. • Intellectual property, workforce and retirement, tariffs, debt issues, etc.
SOCIAL AND CULTURAL SHIFTS, E.G.	• Social policy, redefinition of families, redefinition of morality, spirituality, assimilation, etc. • Discrimination, divided countries, religious extremism, etc.
POLITICAL CONDITIONS, E.G.	• Election issues, federalism and independence, conflicts, etc.

Learn more looking at some official government reports[6] on global mega-trends.

The key to managing complexity is to understand which ones are likely to have a significant impact on the company and market, over the time horizon of the company strategy. Experts insights on the key industry-specific drivers also help shortlist key trends.

6. https://www.eea.
europa.eu/themes/
sustainability-
transitions/global-
megatrends

https://www.dni.gov/
files/documents/nic/
GT-Full-Report.pdf

KNOWN VS. UNKNOWN

The direction and pace of some trends can reasonably be assumed to be known. These provide the "**future background**" for the strategy definition — e.g. we know that machine learning and artificial intelligence are becoming standard in data management and will soon impact in one way or another all customer interactions.

For each of the other trends, it is important to **understand what the actual uncertainty** is:

- Is it the **direction** that will be taken? E.g. will nuclear energy capacity increase or reduce?
- And/or is it the **pace** of change? E.g. how quickly will 5G become standard for mobile data in European countries?

Articulating what the **possible outcomes** for each of these uncertainties are allows to define **scenarios**.

This methodology was first applied by Shell in the 1970s and continues to be part of the company scenario planning approach. You can learn a lot more by searching online "Shell Scenarios".

Note: it is usually more insightful to think through scenarios with uncertainties on the direction, as these could lead to significantly different environments.

BUILD INTO THE STRATEGY

With a set of plausible scenarios agreed on, it is then possible to articulate the company strategy: do we bet the future will head towards scenario A, and we focus 100% of our efforts to win there, or are we conservative and define a "consensus strategy" that should be somehow successful regardless of whether we head towards the scenario A, B or C.

Lastly, it is important to keep in mind that the world is not fully continuous, and some **disruptions occur**. These can fundamentally make scenarios and strategies obsolete. Part of the strategic thinking exercise is to brainstorm these and outline what the company response could be.

MONITORING THE FUTURE

It is helpful to think about the **signs** that indicate we are **going in one direction or another**.

These signs can then be monitored and help the company sense-check whether the strategy is the right one or whether a refresh should be conducted to align with the new reality.

Some companies now leverage artificial intelligence to process big data (e.g. news articles, market prices etc.) and automate this monitoring.

BU PERFORMANCE
KEY SALES PERFORMANCE METRICS

Sales & Market Share	Sales Growth & CAGR	Gross-to-Net Sales	Customer Satisfaction

E.g. Net Promoter Score, Reviews

SALES AND MARKET SHARE

Sales and Market Share are the key metrics reflecting the attractiveness of the company value[7] offering(s) for customers, compared to other alternatives:

> **SALES = VOLUME * PRICE**
>
> **VALUE SHARE = SALES/MARKET SIZE**

It is critical to understand **how these two sales drivers evolve** for the company compared to the whole market – also looking at year-on-year growth – **to understand** the market and competitive positioning **dynamics**[8]:

- Declining sales but stable market share reflects a diminishing market (in value).
- Stable sales but diminishing market share reflects a growing market with a less appealing offering vs. competitors on average.

SALES GROWTH AND CAGR

Sales performance is at the simplest level measured by the growth rate:

- Year-over-year (YoY)
- Over time (Compound Annual Growth Rate or CAGR).

$$\text{CAGR } \%_{\text{n to p}} = \left(\frac{\text{Value}_{\text{year p}}}{\text{Value}_{\text{year n}}} \right)^{\left(\frac{1}{p-n} \right)} - 1$$

GROSS-TO-NET SALES

The Gross-to-Net Sales ratio indicates whether there is an issue with price realization (i.e. a significant gap between the target price and the realized price).

Poor key account management (with disproportionate discounts) is the most common cause, but quality issues can also impact this ratio.

$$\text{GTN } \% = \frac{\text{Net Sales}}{\text{Gross Sales}}$$

where Net sales = Gross Sales – Sales Allowance[9] – Discounts – Returns

7. Keep in mind that in many industries there are different types of sales (gross sales, net sales) and different prices (wholesale price, retail recommended price — with or without VAT), which can skew the value picture.

8. Other performance metrics – correlated with sales to some extent – can be tracked, e.g. customer satisfaction (% or Net Promoter Score — NPS).

9. Sales allowance = discount offered due to quality or shipment issue.

KEY OPERATING PERFORMANCE METRICS

Profit & Cash Management	Return on Assets	Sustainability

Level of service	Level/Utilization Rate	Asset sustainability
Profitability	Effectiveness	Risk management
Cash > 0	Costs	

A DAY-TO-DAY VIEW OF OPERATING PERFORMANCE

A starting point to assess operating performance is to **make sure that**:

- **The company meets its target level of service** (speed – quality – flexibility) for key activities (see page 88).
- **The operating model is profitable overall** i.e. sales minus variable costs (e.g. COGS) remain higher than fixed costs (e.g. rent).
- **The cash flow cycle is healthy** i.e. the cash in the bank remains positive, to be able to pay money owed (see page 120).

AN EXECUTIVE VIEW OF OPERATING PERFORMANCE

We can think about operating performance in a more holistic manner, and **aim to optimize Return on Assets** (see page 90) answering these **3 interdependent questions** (and setting KPIs for each):

- **Are assets sufficiently utilized** (just enough spare capacity and flexibility)?
- **Are the assets effective** (producing enough outputs at the right quality level)?
- **Is the cost of assets optimal** (cost per asset in line or below industry cost)?

SUSTAINABILITY

Sustainability performance dimensions (often correlated with long-term operating expenses) must be considered, in addition to the above metrics, e.g.:

- **Asset sustainability**, for instance employee retention (e.g. churn, employee satisfaction score...) or environmental impact (e.g. % of recycled inputs).
- **Risk management**, for instance employee safety (e.g. number of incidents), or compliance (e.g. share of suppliers audited).

CHEAT SHEET
GROWING PROFITABLY IN A MARKET

DRIVING THE TOP LINE

3 Customers can be SEGMENTED and PRIORITIZED, based on their distinct features, behaviors, and business potential.

4 To be adopted and successful, the VALUE PROPOSITION must be COMPELLING, COMMUNICATED and ACCESSIBLE for target segments.

5 Companies define the ROLE(S) they want to play in the value chain (vs. PARTNERS) to deliver this winning value proposition to target customers, as well as their PROFIT MODEL.

PRICING DEEP-DIVE

Pricing requires to define the TARGET PRICE as well as the PRICE STRUCTURE, visible to customers.

When the price is not regulated, VALUE-BASED pricing allows to compare alternative price-volume scenarios and optimize profit.

ECOSYSTEM MAP

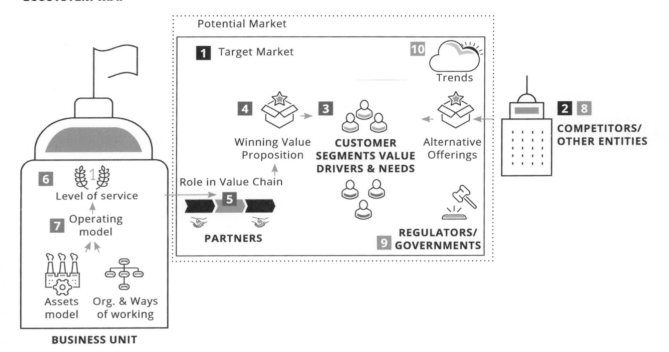

OPTIMIZING THE BOTTOM LINE

6 **Companies must STREAMLINE ACTIVITIES – removing non-value-adding activities – and define the right LEVEL OF SERVICE for key activities, in line with the value proposition.**

7 **This should cascade into the OPERATING MODEL (also impacting companies' CULTURE):**
- **With the right ASSETS MODEL (Return on Assets tradeoffs)**
- **And the appropriate ORG. STRUCTURE and WAYS OF WORKING.**

CHEAT SHEET
KEY OPTIONS TO REMEMBER

A. WHERE TO/HOW TO GROW?

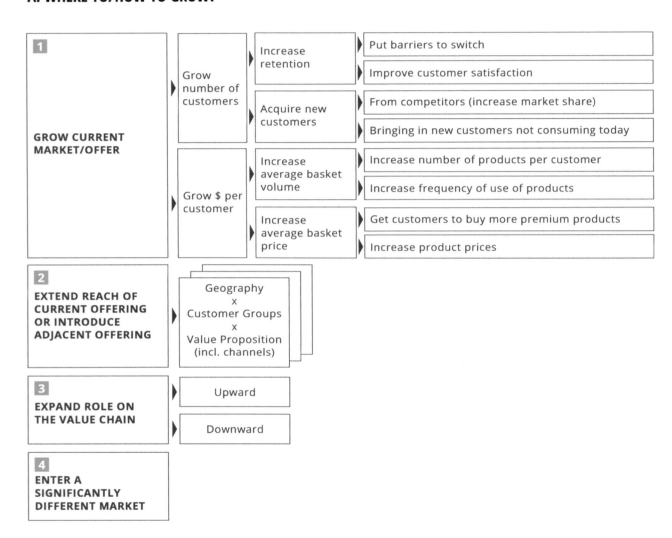

1

GROW CURRENT MARKET/OFFER

- Grow number of customers
  - Increase retention
    - Put barriers to switch
    - Improve customer satisfaction
  - Acquire new customers
    - From competitors (increase market share)
    - Bringing in new customers not consuming today
- Grow $ per customer
  - Increase average basket volume
    - Increase number of products per customer
    - Increase frequency of use of products
  - Increase average basket price
    - Get customers to buy more premium products
    - Increase product prices

2

EXTEND REACH OF CURRENT OFFERING OR INTRODUCE ADJACENT OFFERING

- Geography
  x
  Customer Groups
  x
  Value Proposition
  (incl. channels)

3

EXPAND ROLE ON THE VALUE CHAIN

- Upward
- Downward

4

ENTER A SIGNIFICANTLY DIFFERENT MARKET

HOW TO USE THE GROWTH ISSUE TREE?

Always start with the strategic options on the left (highest level) and define which branches are relevant, before getting one level more granular.

B. HOW TO PRACTICALLY EXECUTE/IMPLEMENT THIS?

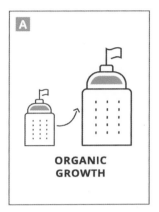

A

ORGANIC GROWTH

B

MERGER & ACQUISITION (M&A)

C

JOINT-VENTURE/ ALLIANCE

CHAPTER 6
CORPORATE STRATEGY
ADDITIONAL CONSIDERATIONS AND VALUE-CREATING DECISIONS AT THE CORPORATE LEVEL

 We have defined in the previous chapter the key components of Business Unit Strategy. The aim of a **Business Unit Strategy** is to **compete and win in a defined market, over time**.

Corporate Strategy, on the other hand, aims to **maximize value creation across multiple markets and Business Units**.

This requires to make **CHOICES** on:

1. The **FINANCIAL STRATEGY,** including financing and shareholding — and their implications on management and governance.

2. The **PORTFOLIO** of sectors and markets to play in.

3. The **ORGANIZATIONAL STRUCTURE** of the company.

We will in this chapter provide an overview of these **3 corporate choices.**

CORPORATE STRATEGY

=

MAXIMIZING VALUE CREATION

FINANCIAL STRATEGY

The Chief Financial Officer (CFO) is responsible for setting the financial strategy of the company, i.e. the three ROE components on the right-hand side of the ROE equation (see next page).

Many corporate finance and management books would be required to properly cover these three components. Luckily, **you do not need to be a finance expert to succeed at strategy interviews**.

Strategy and management consultants primarily focus on Business Strategy, while financial advisory companies help on the Financial Strategy side. Here are **a few financial choices you need be aware of.**

---

3 CAPITAL STRUCTURE

CHOICE 1: LEVEL OF DEBT

The CFO can decide whether the capital is funded by equity or debt. "Gearing" is the share of debt, relative to the amount of equity.

> **GEARING = DEBT/EQUITY**

The higher the gearing, the higher the debt interests to be paid and the higher the risk of debt default.

The benefit on the other hand is that high debt means that very little private equity is required, limiting the shareholders' risk. Another way to look at it is that, with the same amount of equity, an investor can avoid ownership dilution (owning more than 50% of the company shares and the associated voting rights) thanks to debt.

In addition, as debt interests are paid before taxes, as long as the debt interest rate is reasonable, a high-level of indebtment allows to pay less taxes.

Private Equity firms acquire companies this way (via Leveraged Buy Out – LBO –, Management Buy-Out – MBO –, etc.). This enables them to control a company with limited equity and to maximize ROE (higher earnings/low equity).

This only works if the company delivers steady cash flows to pay back the debt. Banks lending to private equity put in place "**covenants**" i.e. thresholds for financial metrics to not breach (e.g. debt-to-equity, minimum EBITDA, fixed-charge coverage ratio etc.), and management obligations (e.g. abide by the law).

If the company breaches a covenant, penalties occur. For instance the borrower may need to add equity, or the interests rate may increase. As a worst case, the loan must be repaid.

CHOICE 2: PUBLIC VS PRIVATE EQUITY

Companies can seek capital by becoming **public listed** – through an IPO – and selling shares to the market or by remaining unlisted seeking private capital (**private equity**).

As mentioned previously, public listed companies need to balance multiple stakeholders' interests and must provide significant **transparency to the market** to allow a fair share valuation.

Corporate Governance thus aims at defining responsibilities – especially around decision-making – for the management of the group.[1]

Governance structures vary from one country to another but they usually distinguish the **Executive Committee**[2] – in charge of daily operations – from the **Board** — mostly non-Executives, representing shareholders.

The competency, personality and integrity of the Executives, as well as the cohesion of the **Executive Team** are key factors **evaluated during M&A processes** as they highly impact the company's ability to create value.

Business Strategy & Operating Model   **Financial Strategy**

$$ROE = \frac{Sales}{Capital\ Employed} \times \frac{Earnings\ Before\ Interests\ \&\ Tax}{Sales} \times \frac{Capital\ Employed}{Equity} \times \frac{Earnings\ Before\ Tax}{Earnings\ Before\ Interests\ \&\ Tax} \times \frac{Earnings\ After\ Tax}{Earnings\ Before\ Tax}$$

Asset Turnover	Operating Margin	CAPITAL STRUCTURE	FINANCIAL COST RATIO	CORPORATE TAX RATE
1	**2**	**3**	**4**	**5**

4 FINANCIAL COST

CHOICE 3: DEBT STRUCTURE & WACC

Structuring the debt with long-term – expensive – , medium-term and short-term – less expensive – debt allows to optimize the cost of debt while providing some flexibility should the company performance improve or decline.

This **cost of debt directly feeds into the Weighted Average Cost of Capital** (WACC see page 60), used to evaluate the company value creation[3].

We will also use the WACC in the following chapter on Valuation.

5 CORPORATE TAXES

CHOICE 4: FOOTPRINT & LEGAL STRUCTURE

Companies pay corporate taxes on Earnings Before Tax.

In principles, corporate taxes are paid where the company is registered. Many companies have thus set up a parent holding company, registered in a country or state with lower corporate tax rates, and nest under it their local subsidiaries (fully owned by the holding company).

Earnings are consolidated at the holding level and the lower corporate tax rate is applied there.

1. These are summarized in "Charters" or "Terms of Reference".

2. Executive Committee roles can vary, but the ones listed below are frequently appointed:

- CEO: Chief Executive Officer
- CFO: Chief Financial Officer
- COO: Chief Operating Officer
- CHRO: Chief Human Resources Officer
- CSO: Chief Strategy Officer
- CMO: Chief Marketing Officer
- CIO: Chief Information Officer
- CISO: Chief Information Security Office.

3. Return Spread = ROCE – WACC

PORTFOLIO MANAGEMENT AND VALUE CREATION

To maximize short- and long-term value, companies often decide to invest in multiple geographies or businesses, reaping the profit in an established market and investing in other promising markets. It gives them a "corporate portfolio", which must be managed. You may have heard for instance of annual "portfolio reviews".

STRATEGIC BUSINESS SEGMENTS

The portfolio is divided into **"Strategic Business Segments" (SBS)**, distinct enough to be in theory manageable independently (there may still be synergies between SBS).

SBS are often translated into the org. model with the creation of Business Units (e.g. Airbus Aircraft, Helicopters, Space, etc.).

PORTFOLIO REVIEW STEPS

1 SBS/BU PROFILING

Conducting a portfolio review starts by looking at each strategic business segment/business unit independently, to evaluate:

1. **Its performance and sustainability:**
   — Is the **industry attractive** (growing and profitable, with no major and disruptive trends or regulatory risks)?
   — Is the SBS/BU's **competitive performance satisfactory and with a promising outlook**, considering competitive dynamics and the planned growth opportunities?

2. **Its value in the company portfolio vs. standalone:**
   — **Strategic fit:** is there a compelling narrative to explain why this SBS/BU belongs to the company, considering the rest of the portfolio. Does this align with the company's vision and ambition?
   — **Synergies**: are we generating growth and efficiency synergies by having this SBS/BU (e.g. shared customer insights or shared back-office center)?

3. **Its risk profile**, e.g. is it capital intensive and very sensitive to market fluctuations? Is it at risk in some of the future scenarios considered?

2 PORTFOLIO REVIEW

The group then looks at the overall portfolio, in steps, to ensure it maximizes the value creation:

1. Evaluate the magnitude of the **negative conglomerate discount**[4] and understand which parts of the business drive this.

2. **Some parts of the business will be identified as value destroying[5]. These must be addressed**:
   — **Core businesses** representing a large share of the revenue **should be turned around.**
   — **Non-core businesses should be divested** (possibly after a turnaround to improve the market value).

3. **Articulate the company investment thesis**:
   — Clarifying **value creation priorities** for each SBS i.e.
     a. Pursue SBS/BU revenue growth.
     b. Fund the growth of other SBS/BUs.
     c. Improve SBS/BU margin.
   — Clarifying the **risk profile** of each business.

3 VALUE CREATION GOALS

Each BU then gets assigned a target KPI aligned with its value creation priority, e.g.:

- Target growth rate
- Target Free Cash Flows (FCF — see next chapter on Valuation)
- Target EBITDA.

In addition, the **return spread (ROCE – WACC)** is worth tracking in each BU – when feasible – to understand the level of value creation or destruction.

Lastly, additional value creation programmes are scoped and initiated at the corporate and BU levels to support the realignment of the portfolio, e.g. divestment, cost reduction program, etc.

4. A BU belonging to a corporate group is usually undervalued by the market, to reflect the fact that its performance is merged with other BUs, and is thus less transparent and liquid than a sole company.

5. Negative return spread i.e. ROCE - WACC <0

ORG. STRUCTURE/MODEL AND ORG. DESIGN

Corporate groups operating in multiple markets can organize their activities in many ways. They can also evolve as their environment, strategy and imperatives change.

The organization design process consists in defining how the company is organized, outlining respective functional scopes, business objectives, budgets and KPIs, decision-making responsibilities, and organizational chart (roles and hierarchy) for business units, relative to the corporate office.

LEADING DIMENSION(S)

Assuming the company is relatively complex, with several offers for different customers and presence in several geographies, **the key challenge is to define which of the dimensions takes priority over others – see examples on the next page –, hence driving the organizational structure.**

MATRIX/HYBRID ORGANISATIONS

Companies can use one dimension or several – matrix – e.g. Geography and Function, with some roles simultaneously reporting to two Managers. This avoids "silo-ing" the organization but can also generate ambiguity and pressure on individuals.

Companies can also have **hybrid** models with different approaches for different products or geographies.

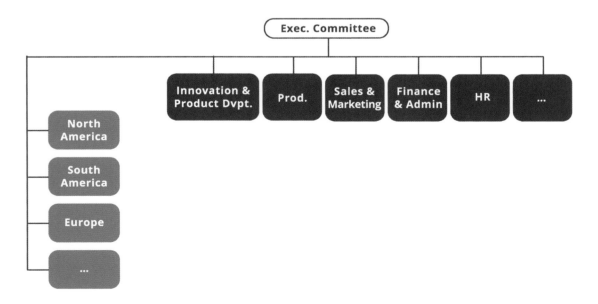

EXAMPLES OF ORG. STRUCTURES WITH DIFFERENT LEADING DIMENSIONS

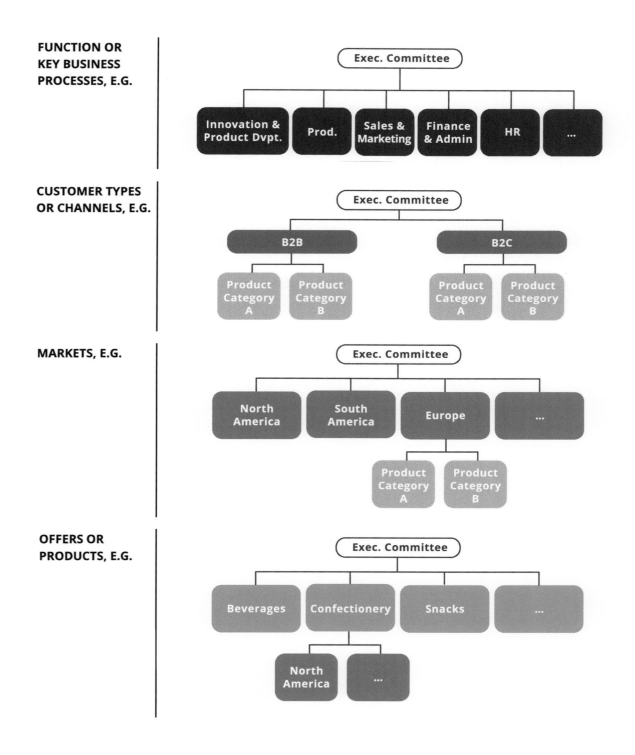

FUNCTION OR KEY BUSINESS PROCESSES, E.G.

Exec. Committee
- Innovation & Product Dvpt.
- Prod.
- Sales & Marketing
- Finance & Admin
- HR
- ...

CUSTOMER TYPES OR CHANNELS, E.G.

Exec. Committee
- B2B
  - Product Category A
  - Product Category B
- B2C
  - Product Category A
  - Product Category B

MARKETS, E.G.

Exec. Committee
- North America
- South America
- Europe
  - Product Category A
  - Product Category B
- ...

OFFERS OR PRODUCTS, E.G.

Exec. Committee
- Beverages
- Confectionery
  - North America
  - ...
- Snacks
- ...

EVALUATING ALTERNATIVE ORG. MODEL OPTIONS

We listed previously in **BU Strategy – Bottom Line** a set of **diagnostic questions** to help list and assess alternative **operating model options for a specific SBS/BU** (see page 92).

At the corporate level, we need to conduct a **similar diagnosis, but looking simultaneously at all the strategic business segments** in the portfolio and **answering in addition the questions below on the opportunity or need for centralization.**

 DIAGNOSIS – "AS IS"

ANSWER THE 6 BU-LEVEL OP. MODEL DIAGNOSTIC QUESTIONS (SEE PAGE 92)...

...AS WELL AS THESE CORPORATE LEVEL DIAGNOSTIC QUESTIONS:

 If managed independently, would we have strategic business segments/BUs with SIGNIFICANTLY DIFFERENT OPERATING MODELS?

If so, is it key to enable coordination: Intra-BU? Across BUs? Across geographies? Externally with partners?
What level of culture and values alignment is needed and how is it enabled?

 Are there CROSS-BU AND/OR CROSS-GEOGRAPHY EFFICIENCY SYNERGIES (e.g. cost reduction, resource utilization)?

If yes, are they significant enough to justify embedding in the org. structure, e.g. with global business services, centers of excellence, or even by making them BUs/geographies?

 Is it necessary and feasible to have CENTRALIZED DECISION-MAKING AND CONTROL?
At which level in the organization should decision-making sit regarding for instance:

Strategy and Finance
- Strat plan definition and strategic reviews; M&As
- Financial strategy, shareholders relationships and corporate governance (e.g. updates to the Board for public-listed companies)
- P&L accountability (incl. financial KPIs).

Marketing
- Is it critical to have a strong corporate brand and unified communications at the corporate level?

Operations
- Infrastructure management
- Procurement and supply chain management
- Corporate ways of working.

IT
- Data management
- Assets and systems procurement, development and maintenance.

Compliance/Risk management
- Where does responsibility sit and who has the final say for a risky decision? How is this enforced?

HR
- Performance management and incentives
- Career and mobility.

Corporate affairs/Legal
- Who can represent the company publicly?
- Who can sign contracts (with which thresholds)?

   **DIAGNOSIS**
       "AS IS"   →   **ORG. MODEL DESIGN**
                                         "TO BE"

Once you have completed this diagnosis, with answers to BU and corporate-level questions, you should be able to **start the design phase of the org. design** process. In this phase, you will most likely consider, compare and prioritize multiple org. model options, before becoming more granular.

    ORG. MODEL DESIGN – "TO BE"

EXAMPLE ORG. DESIGN METHOD

1 **Outline the CORE MINIMUM CENTRAL GOVERNANCE bodies** and functions, based on decisions that need to be made at the central level.

2 **Select the additional SYNERGIES TO LEVERAGE** across the portfolio (e.g. Center of Excellence, Global Shared Services).

3 **Define the primary and secondary org. dimensions** and derive a **HIGH-LEVEL ORG. STRUCTURE** (see page 114). You will likely come up with **multiple scenarios**.

Outline **key accountabilities** in each scenario.

4 **Clarify the corporate WAYS OF WORKING For the selected high-level org. structure,** vertically (between layers) and horizontally (across each layer).

Start outlining the more detailed org. chart.

CHAPTER 7
VALUATION
AN INTRODUCTION TO THE KEY PROJECT AND COMPANY VALUATION CONCEPTS AND METHODS

Many business decisions require to conduct a **valuation** to understand whether it is worth investing in a project or company.

We can value many things, e.g. an R&D **project**, a plant building project or a **company acquisition**.

We will introduce in this chapter a few ways to value these, but we will beforehand cover **corporate finance pre-requisites: cash flows and free cash flows (FCF).**

LOOK FOR
CASH
FLOWS

CASH FLOW MANAGEMENT

CASH INFLOW

Operations, e.g.:

- Sales of the offer(s) e.g. goods, services, license right.

Company financing, e.g.:

- Subscribed loans (short or long term)
- Shares issued
- Bonds issued.

Divestments & return on investment, e.g.:

- Sales of assets
- Interests/principal for money lent to others
- Dividends received for other company's shares/bonds owned.

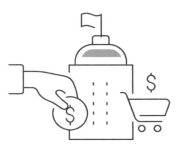

CASH OUTFLOW

Operating expenses, e.g.:

- Raw material
- Utilities
- Third party providers
- Sales & Marketing
- Overheads (support and admin)
- Taxes.

Financing costs, e.g.:

- Debt principal repayment and interest payment
- Dividend payment to shareholders.

Investments, e.g.:

- Capital expenditure
- Acquisitions.

While the overall objective of a company is to create value, the company needs to ensure it holds enough cash to operate on a daily basis.

The treasury and finance department forecasts and checks the **net cash position**, which is the **difference between cash inflows and outflows**.

CASH FLOW STATEMENT

This information is summarized every year in the Statement of Cash Flows (the third key financial statement produced at least once a year — see next page).

WORKING CAPITAL REQUIREMENT

On a daily basis, companies aim to minimize the working capital requirement (WCR) i.e. the cash needed to pay suppliers' invoices until they receive clients' payments.

The lower the WCR, the lower the likelihood to disrupt operations due to a lack of cash, and the higher the cash that can be reinvested to keep growing the business.

Note: payment terms for Payables (suppliers) and Receivables (clients) have a significant impact on the working capital requirement.

SIMPLIFIED CASH FLOW STATEMENT

Company A
Statement of Cash Flows
1st January year n – 1st January n+1

Cash at Start of Period

Cash Flows from Operating Activities

+ Earnings after tax

+ Depreciation expense

– Change in working capital requirements

1 Net Cash Flows from Operating Activities

Cash Flows from Investing Activities

+ Sale of fixed assets

– Capital expenditures and acquisitions

2 Net Cash Flows from Investing Activities

Cash Flows from Financing Activities

+ Increase in long-term borrowings

+ Increase in short-term borrowings

– Long-term debt repaid

– Dividend payments

3 Net Cash Flows from Financing Activities

Total Net Cash Flows = **1** + **2** + **3**

Cash at End of Period = Cash at Start of Period + Total Net Cash Flows

FREE CASH FLOWS (FCF)

> **FCF = OPERATING CASH – CAPITAL EXPENDITURE (CAPEX)**
>
> = EBIT (1 – TAX RATE) + D&A – CHANGES IN WORKING CAPITAL – NET CAPEX
>
> ◄·············· From P&L ··············► ◄·············· From Balance Sheet ··············►

With Net Capex = YoY change in fixed assets + depreciation/amortization

---

As mentioned in the previous chapters, the financial performance (ROE) is the result of five components:

1. Asset turnover
2. Operating margin
3. Capital structure
4. Financial cost ratio
5. Corporate tax rate

When considering an investment, **some** of these **components are not intrinsic** to the project, e.g.:

- Corporate tax rate depends on the holding company location.
- Financial cost depends on the investors' financing model (e.g. replacing equity with debt).

Investors thus calculate a specific metric called Free Cash Flow – FCF – to understand the level of positive or negative cash flows that the target investment (project or company) may intrinsically generate over time.

To do this they take all the cash flows, with the exception of:

- Cash flows related to **financing** – e.g. debt interests – as these can be changed with another financing model.
- Cash flows related to **corporate taxes**, as a different company structure could change the tax rate and accounting mechanisms.

This is equivalent to looking at how much a company generates after paying for capital expenditures (capex) and reflects its capacity to invest in additional opportunities.

Note: negative FCF is not necessarily a bad sign. It may just reflect the fact that the company is conducting investments.

Capex-intensive industries (e.g. utilities) usually generate low or negative FCF due to high capital expenditures.

NET PRESENT VALUE (NPV) & PROJECT VALUATION

$$DCF = \frac{CF_{\text{year }1}}{(1+rate)^1} + \frac{CF_{\text{year }2}}{(1+rate)^2} + \ldots + \frac{CF_{\text{year }n}}{(1+rate)^n}$$

$$NPV = CF_{\text{year }0} + DCF$$

The NPV approach considers that a project value is equal to the "present value" of future free cash flows.

NET PRESENT VALUE AND DCF

Let's first look at an example to understand the concept of "net present value":

Assuming the WACC is 10%, USD 100 should yield USD 110 in a year.

If you think about it the other way round, USD 110 in a year are worth USD 100 today (= USD 110/(1+10%)).

A very common application of this is dealing with inflation. If all prices increase by 2% per year, I will need 2% more next year (USD 30,600) to buy the car I could buy today for USD 30,000. USD 30,600 next year are equivalent to USD 30,000 today, because I get the same asset.

Every year, we divide by (1 + rate). This division is called "Discounting the Cash Flow" (DCF method).

Consequently, if we know the future free cash flows of a project (negative e.g. upfront investment, operating expenses and positive e.g. sales), we can **calculate the NPV by summing all the free cash flows,** discounted year after year over the valuation period, **including the initial cash flow in the start year (negative in case of an investment).**

NPV AND IRR

Companies usually use the WACC as the rate to discount projects, seeking a positive return spread: Return – WACC > 0.

If the NPV is positive, the project is creating value compared to the target set by the WACC.

If the NPV is negative, the project is not creating enough value and it should probably not be undertaken.

You may hear as well about the **Internal Rate of Return (IRR)**. It is the **discount rate that makes the NPV calculation equal to 0**.

- If the IRR is superior to the WACC, the project creates enough value.
- If it is lower than the WACC, it does not create enough value.

COMPANY VALUATION METHODS

When companies acquire another entity or divest one of their BU, it must be valued to set a selling price or make an offer. This process is called "valuation"

Three main valuation approaches are used:

1. **Asset-based**
2. **Cash flow-based (DCF/NPV)**
3. **Market-/comparator-/multiples-based.**

None of them will give you the right answer. Strategy practitioners will consider that the reality is somewhere in the middle. You should thus apply and **triangulate different methods to define a realistic value range.**

Very different values should be a warning sign and should entice you to review and **refine assumptions**.

1 ASSET BASED

Different methods exist to do the asset-based valuation. The most common is the **Net Realizable Value**, which represents the **value left after selling the assets** (i.e. deducting the cost of disposing of them).

> **NET REALIZABLE VALUE =**
>
> **NET TANGIBLE ASSETS - LIABILITIES**

It is **by no means a good way to value a company**, as it does not fully reflect the company value (which is more than the sum of its assets and could include intangible assets e.g. goodwill).

However, it is helpful as it gives an indication of the **minimum value** under which the company should not be sold.

2 CASH FLOW BASED

This is probably the most "scientific" approach to value a company, but it is highly dependent on the quality of the forecast for growth and cash flows.

Example: if we have a forecast of free cash flows for the next 3 years:

- We must determine what will be the **value of the company beyond this horizon (the "terminal value").**
- If we assume the company will keep growing at a constant growth rate k:

$$\text{Terminal Value} = \text{FCF}_{\text{final year}} \times \frac{(1+k)}{\text{WACC} - k}$$

- An alternative approach exists and is similar to the market multiple valuation approach (see next column) based on the EBITDA in the last year:

$$\text{Terminal Value} = \text{EBITDA}_{\text{final year}} \times (\text{EBITDA multiple})$$

- The net present value is then equal to the discounted cash flows over the forecast horizon – 3 years in this example – plus the terminal value:

$$\text{NPV} = \text{DCF} + \text{TV}$$

3 MULTIPLES BASED

The general idea is to define a "peer group" of companies with a similar profile (same industry/portfolio, size, positioning, etc.) and **look at the history of transactions or market performance, to then extrapolate the value of your target.**
There are two "families" of valuation variations, which differ by the financial ratio used.

1. **Option 1 is to use equity price multiples.** This is for instance helpful for share acquisition.
   — **P/E Ratio** (price per share divided by earnings per share) is the quick and standard metric.
   — **Multiply target's earnings by the average P/E ratio** in the peer group to define the estimated equity value.

2. **Option 2 is to use the Enterprise Value multiples** (EV = Market Capitalisation + Debt), to evaluate the fair market value. This is for instance used in M&A.
   — **EV/EBITDA is the most commonly used ratio** as it is not impacted by the companies' accounting choices regarding depreciation and amortization. This is helpful in particular to evaluate a company in a capex-intensive industry.
   — Other frequently used multiples are EV/EBIT and EV/FCF.

KNOWLEDGE

QUIZ

STRATEGY & FINANCE KNOWLEDGE QUIZ
I. ECOSYSTEM MAP

Draw in the frame below the 10 components of the ecosystem map and number each component to reflect the logic outlined in the Business Strategy chapter.

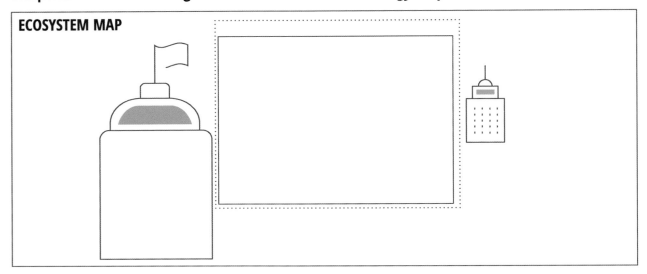

ECOSYSTEM MAP

Double check on the Ecosystem Map page 68 that you have listed the right components.

Describe below a sector and company you are familiar with, using the 10 components of the Ecosystem Map.

Industry / ecosystem: ☐   Company: ☐

1. ....

2. ....

3. ....

4. ....

5. ....

6. ....

7. ....

8. ....

9. ....

10. ....

STRATEGY & FINANCE KNOWLEDGE QUIZ
II. "WHERE TO/HOW TO" GROWTH ISSUE TREE

Draw in the frame below the growth issue tree.

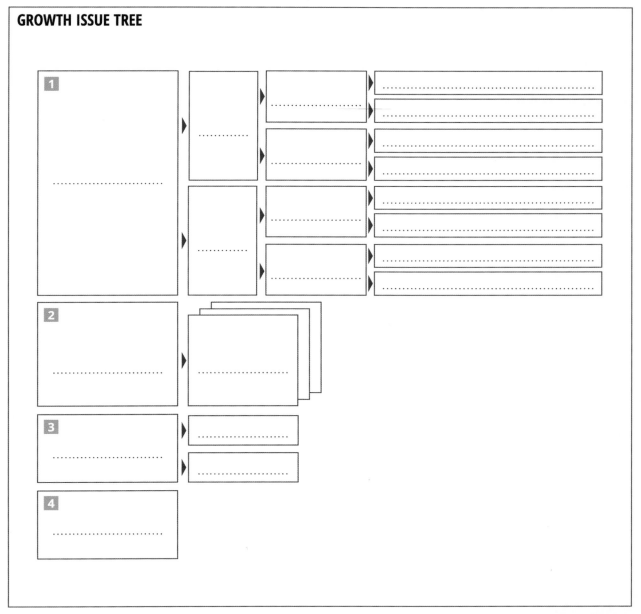

Review the growth issue tree page 66.

STRATEGY & FINANCE KNOWLEDGE QUIZ
III. STRATEGY AND OPERATIONS QUIZ

What are the 3 things to check in the value proposition if there is a top line issue?

See Winning Value Proposition page 78.

What are the key steps of the pricing algorithm?

> **What pricing strategy should be applied?**
> ↓

See Pricing Algorithm page 84.

What are the 2 key components of an operating model?

See Operating Model page 89.

What are the 3 main types of assets?

What are the return on assets tradeoffs?

See Return on Assets Tradeoffs page 90.

What are the potential roles of a government?

See "Regulators, Governments and Public Service page 98.

What are the 3 categories of corporate strategy choices?

See Corporate Strategy page 108.

STRATEGY & FINANCE KNOWLEDGE QUIZ
IV. FINANCE QUIZ

What are the key elements in a P&L?

Company A
Profit & Loss Statement (P&L)
1st January year n – 31st December year n+1

....

\- ....

= ....

\- ....

= ....

\- ....

= ....

\- ....

\- ....

= ....

\- ....

= ....

See Simplified Profit & Loss (P&L) page 58.

What are the 5 components of the ROE?

$$\text{ROE} = \boxed{} \times \boxed{} \times \boxed{} \times \boxed{} \times \boxed{}$$

....

See Maximizing Investor Value page 61.

What is the formula of the return spread?

RETURN SPREAD = [_____] − [_____]

See Company Value-Add page 60.

How to calculate FCF?

FCF = [___] × ([___] − [___]) + [___] − [___] − [___]

See "Free Cash Flows (FCF) page 122.

What is the CAGR over this time period?
What is the year-over-year growth between 2017 and 2018?

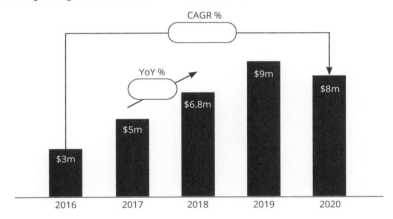

See Key Sales Performance Metrics page 102.
Answers at the bottom of this page.

What is the NPV for the project below?

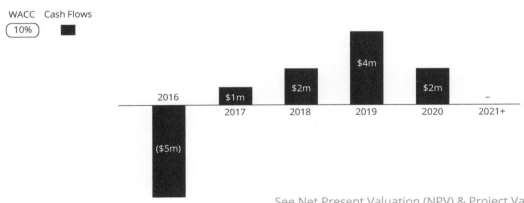

See Net Present Valuation (NPV) & Project Valuation page 123.
Answers at the bottom of this page.

CAGR % ≈ 27.8%; YoY % ≈ +36%; NPV ≈ +$1.93m.

PROBLEM
SOLVING

CHAPTER 8
SOLVING BLOCKS METHOD
HOW TO CONFIDENTLY START, STRUCTURE AND SOLVE A STRATEGY CASE

There are a lot of critical misconceptions about how to start a case study, spread on the Internet or by other candidates, e.g.:

1. "When I listen to an interviewer, I must request one minute to think about a structure…"
2. "… then I need to play back the question I heard…"
3. "…and propose a structure. For this I will pick one of the 10 frameworks I have learnt by heart and list all the questions or topics covered in the framework".

These are **3 wrong tactics aiming to avoid an awkward gap** at the beginning of the case.

You can easily avoid these gaps by being methodical and aligning on the best solving approach with the interviewer (instead of magically giving the "right answer").

Consultants do not know the answer when they first hear about a client problem.

They ask questions and build an approach, combining solving blocks. We will detail this "Solving Blocks" method in this chapter.

ASK

QUESTIONS

SOLVING BLOCKS
HOW CONSULTANTS STRUCTURE APPROACHES

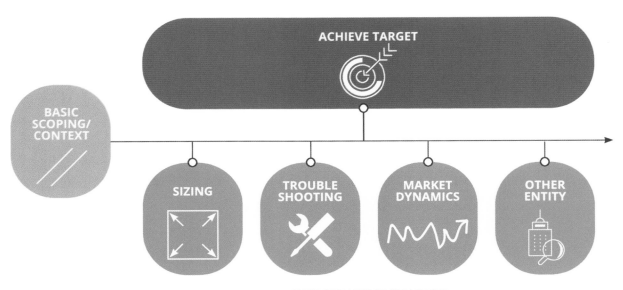

Clients commission strategy consultants to do two main things:

I. IMPROVE UNDERSTANDING **i.e. gain insights into something they do not have the capacity or capability to structure, clarify or analyze internally.**

These questions fall under 4 sub-categories:

1. **SIZING** i.e. estimate a quantity or volume, such as a market size.
2. **TROUBLESHOOTING** i.e. identify the root cause(s) of a problem.
3. **MARKET DYNAMICS** i.e. understand what the driving forces of a market are and how it may evolve in the future, considering key trends.
4. **OTHER ENTITY** i.e. profile another entity – e.g. a competitor, a target company, or a public body – to understand how it operates and what its strategy is.

II. ACHIEVE A TARGET **i.e. consultants help them achieve a business or personal goal.**

We call these problem types or questions **"SOLVING BLOCKS"** as, in order to answer your full client's ask, you may need to **combine and sequence several blocks** — just like building blocks.

In addition to the solving blocks listed above, you will need a **BASIC SCOPING/CONTEXT BLOCK**, at the beginning of each case.

ILLUSTRATION: PUTTING TOGETHER A PROJECT PROPOSAL

Consultants combine solving blocks when they prepare a proposal or deliver a project.

Let's assume a company hopes to prioritize its next market entry, based on market potential. This is an **ACHIEVE TARGET CASE**.

Consultants will put together a proposal that outlines the understanding of the needs and objectives, as well as an approach.

BASIC SCOPING/CONTEXT: prior to writing anything, consultants will have an initial briefing meeting, during which they will have the opportunity to clarify the scope, e.g.:

- Clarify the **context** and the actual **needs and objectives** (it turns out the company seeks to achieve double digit growth in the next 3 years).
- **Define** what **success** would you look like for the project (e.g. a business case for one prioritized market).
- Gather practical information about the project (timelines, key stakeholders to involve).

Only then will they be able to propose a **structured approach** to address the client's needs, e.g.:

--------------------------------- ACHIEVE TARGET ---------------------------------

1 ACHIEVE TARGET SCOPING

Align with team members and Steering Committee on project objectives, scope, and decision-making criteria and constraints.

2 LIST OPTIONS

Conduct an initial brainstorming of potential entry options and customer groups in each market.

3 ASSESS OPTIONS

Conduct primary and secondary market research to evaluate the attractiveness of each market in scope, i.e.:

—— **MARKET DYNAMICS** ——

Insights on consumption, competitive and regulatory dynamics.

—— **SIZING** ——

Sizing of 2-3 key customer segments.

Conduct a preliminary assessment of market entry options, based on criteria agreed upfront.

Facilitate a prioritization workshop with the team.

4 WRAP-UP

Present and endorse recommendation with the Steering Committee.

As you can see in this approach, IMPROVE UNDERSTANDING **blocks** (MARKET DYNAMICS and MARKET SIZING) are **needed** to support decision-making, **within an overarching ACHIEVE TARGET** project. This is an extremely frequent pattern.

We will in the following pages **detail each** IMPROVE UNDERSTANDING **block, before tackling the ACHIEVE TARGET approach.** After most blocks, you will find illustrative **interview dialogues** to give you a sense of how this method can be practically applied in a real interview.

To wrap-up, we will give you **practical tips to start a case**, identify the case type and outline an overarching approach using the solving blocks. You will find **dry run exercises** at the back of this chapter to practice the method, **before practicing with mock interviews**.

"IMPROVE UNDERSTANDING" BLOCKS
SIZING (1/2)

1. SCOPE ALIGNMENT

When the case is framed as a sizing, the **scope alignment** block is not about understanding a business context. It is **focused on defining the key parameters** that delineate your sizing exercise.

All the questions below apply to any sizing and must be answered before laying out anything.

- **What are we trying to quantify?** Count, Size, Area, Volume, Revenue, Profit...?
- **As a total** (in country X, in a company...) or **as an average** (per geography, per household, per individual...)?
- Over which **geographical area** (if multiple countries, consider the sizing unit/currency)?
- **When** or over which time horizon (in 1982, in 2050, this year, over the last 12 months...)?

2. SUBMARKETS

Assess whether the sizing needs to be broken down into submarkets, with structurally **different assumptions** (e.g. different activities and sources of revenue/business models, different regions...).

- E.g. a hairdresser makes money by cutting hair – service – and is also a small retailer — selling professional hair products, with a price markup.

Check with the interviewer whether you need to size all the submarkets.

If the interviewer wants you to size multiple submarkets, **start with the most important submarket first** — you might not have time to tackle others.

3. OVERARCHING EQUATION

Define for each submarket considered the overarching equation leading to the metric you are aiming to calculate. To do this, **break down the metric you aim to quantify as the product of:**

- **A unit of analysis** e.g. a household, a house, an individual
- **A metric (quantity or value),** e.g. number of cars, electricity consumption, etc.

Then, break-down again the quantity or value into sub-components, e.g.:

- Household electricity consumption = number of appliances * average consumption per appliance
  = Number of white appliances * average consumption per white appliance
  - \+ Heating appliances * average consumption per white appliance
  - \+ Smaller appliances * average consumption per white appliance.

The more components in the equation, the longer the sizing exercise so avoid lengthy equations.

Let's illustrate this with the sizing of the dog food market in value in Canada. Start drawing a **summary table with the key components of your equation in columns**. You will populate it as you run your calculations. This will allow you to easily wrap-up your calculations.

	OVERARCHING EQUATION				
	UNIT OF ANALYSIS	x METRIC PER UNIT OF ANALYSIS			
SEGMENTS	Number of households	x average number of dogs	x number of meals/dog/year	x amount of food/ meal (g)	x dog food price ($/g)

4. MEANINGFUL SEGMENTS

Reflect on your equation and think about **key factors influencing the different components**. This should naturally lead you to **identify whether there are different cases/segments** with really significantly different sets of assumptions for the components of the equation.

- E.g. for a hairdresser, men and women is a meaningful way to segment, since we can expect the frequency, duration, complexity, products used and overall cost and profit to differ.

If you define several segments, you need to define the relative distribution of each segment in your total market (e.g. 60% customers female, 40% male).

The more segments, the longer the sizing, so keep things manageable with less than 5 segments.
You may only have one or 2 segments for a simple or back-of-the-envelope sizing.

Add segments as rows to your sizing table:

	OVERARCHING EQUATION				
	UNIT OF ANALYSIS	x METRIC PER UNIT OF ANALYSIS			
SEGMENTS	Number of households	x average number of dogs	x number of meals/dog/year	x amount of food/ meal (g)	x dog food price ($/g)
Metropolitan - affluent					
Metropolitan - other					
Rural with land					
Rural - other					

"IMPROVE UNDERSTANDING" BLOCKS
SIZING (2/2)

---

5. NO. OF UNITS OF ANALYSIS

You can use **two alternative approaches to quantify the number of units of analyses for each segment.**
Each approach encompasses several variations:

1. **"Population" approach:**
    — **Density per area, per city size, etc.** E.g. 27,000 inhabitants per square mile in NYC.
    — **Number of people per age group.** E.g. 1/8 of the total population in each decade.

2. **"Geometric" approach:**
    — **Distance.** E.g. one unit every 200 m.
    — **Area.** E.g. one unit per 1 km^2 in a 10 km^2 city.
    — **Volume.** E.g. volume of a plane divided by the volume of a tennis ball.

Note: the number of units of analysis can be a % of the total (e.g. for an average) or the absolute number for each unit.

6. QUANTIFY UNIT OF ANALYSIS

If your scope includes calculating a metric (e.g. revenue), you need to calculate that metric for one unit of analysis, before multiplying by the number of units you calculated in step 5.

You can apply **two main approaches to quantify the volume or value per unit of analysis:**

1. **"Productive" approach = Available time/Production duration.**
    For example:
    — Unit of analysis: store
    — Metric to quantify: number of sales per store
    — Available time: total store opening hours
    — Production duration: time per sale
    > **Unit of analysis metric = total store opening hours/time per sale.**

2. **"Consumption" approach = Quantity per period * Number of periods.**
   For example:
   — Unit of analysis: household with a baby
   — Metric to quantify: annual number of nappies
   — Quantity per period: 4 per day * 1.5 babies on average
   — Number of periods: 52 weeks
   > **Unit of analysis metric = 4 * 1.5 * 52 = 312 nappies per year.**

If a price is part of the equation, it can be segment-specific or equal across the board.

Looking at our Canadian dog food market sizing table, we could for instance do:

SEGMENTS	OVERARCHING EQUATION				
	UNIT OF ANALYSIS	x METRIC PER UNIT OF ANALYSIS			
	Number of households	x average number of dogs	x number of meals/dog/year	x amount of food/ meals (g)	x dog food price ($/g)
Metropolitan – affluent	Population – Density approach	Consumption approach – avg. no. of dogs across segment households	Consumption approach – average assumption (2.5 meals per day * 365 days/year), assuming similar family patterns and presence at home mid-day across segments.	Consumption approach – average assumption (100 g per meal), assuming a similar mix of breeds across all segments.	Segment-related price assumption
Metropolitan – other	Population – Density approach	Consumption approach – avg. no. of dogs across segment households			Segment-related assumption
Countryside with land	Population – Density approach	Consumption approach – avg. no. of dogs across segment households			Segment-related assumption
Countryside without land	Population – Density approach	Consumption approach – avg. no. of dogs across segment households			Segment-related assumption

Note: this is an illustrative example. Fill-in your table with your calculations (not with the approach). You are free to use a different equation, different segments and different approaches to size cells.

7. WRAP-UP AND SENSE-CHECK

Leverage your summary table to size each row and sum-up across your different segments to wrap-up the sizing. If you did not have time to size all segments, have a try at extrapolating these based on what you have already calculated.

Take a moment to **reflect on the numbers** you come-up with (throughout the case, but also at the end), **sense-checking orders of magnitude (see page 210)**.

"IMPROVE UNDERSTANDING" BLOCKS
SIZING EXAMPLE 1 (1/2)

INTERVIEWER   CANDIDATE

> What is your estimation of the revenue of an IKEA store?

> Where would this store be located (e.g. Europe, US)? Are we looking at the annual/weekly/daily revenue? What year are we looking at?

Clarify and align on the scope:
- Total Revenue for one store (shared by interviewer)
- Over which geographical area?
- When or over which time horizon?

> We are interested in the annual revenue of an IKEA store in Berlin in 2019.

> OK. Let's first list the different sources of revenue of an IKEA store:
>
> 1. Selling flat-pack furniture +
> 2. Operating the restaurant +
> 3. Sales from the cafe and from the small food store after the checkouts.
>
> I guess the store also generates online revenue (e.g. stores may have Click&Collect points or organize deliveries) but as this is not directly related to one particular store, I would put them aside, if you don't mind.

List submarkets (different sources of revenue here) and prioritize them to focus on the most important ones first.

> I agree with you. Let's park aside the online revenue streams and focus on the ones generated in-store. Also, to save time, we will focus on the furniture revenue.

> The revenue derived from the furniture sold in store equals: Number of customers per year * Average basket price.

Fine by me.

	OVERARCHING EQUATION		
	UNIT OF ANALYSIS	x METRIC PER UNIT OF ANALYSIS	=
SEGMENTS	Number of customers	Average furniture basket price	Furniture revenue

Productive approach.

Let's deep dive into the first part of the equation, the number of customers per year. One way to quantify this could be to look at the number of time people go through checkouts, i.e.: **Opening hours per year * Number of open checkouts/ Time per sale.**

1. Opening hours per year = Number of hours open per day* Number of open days:
   — We could differentiate weekdays vs. week-ends but let's take the simplifying assumption of a store being open from 9:00 a.m. to 9:00 p.m. on average, which equals to 12h/day, if that's OK?
   — Number of open days: all year long except some public holidays (Christmas, New Year, Easter, etc.). This should be about 360 days, but if you don't mind, I would round down to 350 for calculation purposes.
   — This gives us 12h/day*350days/year= 4,200 hours/year

2. Number of open checkouts:
   — Based on my experience, I think I have usually seen about 8 self-checkouts and 6 traditional checkouts. That's 14 checkouts. Again for simplification purposes, I would estimate that the 14 checkouts are all open at all times, whenever the store is open.

3. Time per sale:
   — Again, based on my experience, customers will spend 4 to 8 minutes at the checkout so let's say 6 min on average, regardless of the checkout type, customer type, factoring-in that sales are not happening in an uninterrupted way.

Make assumptions based on your personal experience.

"IMPROVE UNDERSTANDING" BLOCKS
SIZING EXAMPLE 1 (2/2)

It is a strong assumption but it feels about right.

For the basket price, we apply here a very basic consumption approach (a more sophisticated sizing could have looked at the furniture needs and the renewal frequency to derive the average spend).

This gives us a number of sales equal to:

Opening hours per year * Number of open checkouts / Time per sale

= 4,200h * 14 checkouts/6 min

= 4,200*60*14/6=588,000 sales/year

Let's look at the second part of our equation: the average basket price. Berlin is a dynamic student city. I could easily imagine that these students are looking for furniture at a reasonable price.

Also, the cost of living is cheaper in Berlin than in other major European cities. I would take an assumption of about EUR 150 on average. Would that work?

Structure your notes in a table to keep track of your assumptions and calculation results.

	OVERARCHING EQUATION		
	UNIT OF ANALYSIS	x METRIC PER UNIT OF ANALYSIS	=
SEGMENTS	Number of customers (number of times people go through checkouts)	Average furniture basket price	Furniture revenue
Any customer	4,200h * 14 checkouts/6 min = 588,000 sales/year	EUR 150	

Let's keep that number. What is your assumption for that store revenue then?

Annual revenue from the furniture sale equals:

Number of sales per year * Average basket price = 588 000 sales/year* EUR 150 = EUR 88m.

Wrap-up calculations and sense-check orders of magnitude — even if the interviewer doesn't ask for it.

OVERARCHING EQUATION		
UNIT OF ANALYSIS	x METRIC PER UNIT OF ANALYSIS	=
SEGMENTS	Number of customers (number of times people go through checkouts)	Average furniture basket price	Furniture revenue
Any customer	4,200h * 14 checkouts/6 min = 588,000 sales/year	EUR 150	88m

What do you think of that number?

Well, at first sight, it seems high. At the same time, IKEA is such a big player in the furniture market, generating dozens of billion euros in revenue. Each store represents an enormous investment in terms of real estate, inventory and staff. IKEA needs to make the most of it to make it profitable. I guess that's why they are located in high-density area, to ensure a continuous flow of customers.

Also, we are talking about revenue here, not profit. Looking at the profit margin would be interesting as well.

Interviewers are looking at your structure and way of thinking more than at the actual results. They may know the real number and share it with you.

Actually, you are about right. In 2019, IKEA generated EUR 41bn in revenue for a bit more than 430 stores. This gives us an average of EUR 95m per store.

"IMPROVE UNDERSTANDING" BLOCKS
SIZING EXAMPLE 2 (1/2)

INTERVIEWER   CANDIDATE

Interviewer: How big was the iPhone market in the US in 2018?

Candidate: Are we looking for the number of units sold or the value that it represents?

Also, should we include the second-hand market in this analysis?

> Clarify and align on the scope:
> - Total 2018 US market (shared by interviewer)
> - Number, Volume, Revenue, Profit?
>
> List the submarkets:
> - New?
> - Second-hand?

Interviewer: We will focus on the number of brand new iPhone units sold in Apple Stores in the US in number, not in value.

Candidate: Great. Thinking about it, the number of iPhones could be broken down as the sum of 2 distinct streams of business:

1. People acquiring a phone for the first time and
2. People replacing their phone.

The US is a relatively mature market regarding smartphones. Sales are primarily driven by phone renewal rather than first time acquisition so if you agree I propose we focus on the second stream.

Interviewer: Agreed. How would you proceed then?

Overarching equation

Unit of analysis: individuals owning a phone.

List influencing factors and derive relevant segments.

Estimate the number of units of analysis for each segment ("population" approach).

The number of iPhones replaced in a year can be defined as:
the total pool of phones * replacement rate * iPhone share =
individuals owning at least one phone * average number of phones they own * average replacement rate * average iPhone share.

I suspect the main factor impacting the number of phones is whether people work full time at a company which subsidizes their professional mobile phone.

I also assume kids under 12 do not own a phone. Similarly I suspect few people aged over 75 have a phone and replace it.

I will thus focus the quantification on 3 segments:

1. Teenagers and students aged ~10-25
2. Professionals aged ~25-60 and
3. People not working or retired and aged ~25-75

Does that make sense?

It does, keep going.

Great. Let's size these segments first. We know that the US population is about 320m people with an average life expectancy of 80 years. This gives us approximately 4m people per year, and hence:

- Segment 1: ~15*4m = 60m.
- Segment 2: ~35*4m = 140m people. We can probably withdraw ~25% either unemployed or working as casuals, which thus gives us 105m people in this segment.
- Segment 3: 320m (US population) – 60m [segment 1] – 105m [segment 2] – 5*4m (75-80 year old) – 10*4m (0-10 year old) =95m.

Let's now quantify the number of phones for each segment.

| SEGMENTS | OVERARCHING EQUATION | | | | |
| | UNIT OF ANALYSIS | x METRIC PER UNIT OF ANALYSIS | | | = |
	Number of people	Number of phones	Replacement rate	iPhone share	Number of iPhones replaced
1) Teenagers/ students, 10-25 yo	60m				
2) Professionals, 25-60 yo	105m				
3) People not working or retired, 25-75 yo	95m				

"IMPROVE UNDERSTANDING" BLOCKS
SIZING EXAMPLE 2 (2/2)

OK

> I will make the following assumptions:
>
> - Segment 1: by the age of 15 I suspect most kids have a phone; under 15 maybe 50% have 1 phone. This would give on average for the 10-25 year old segment $(1/2*5+1*10)/15=5/6$.
> - Segment 2: I assume that person in this segment owns 1 personal phone. Let's say that 1 professional out of 5 gets a company mobile phone. Within these, 1/4 drop their personal phone as they find this more convenient. That means we have $4/5*1 + 1/5*(3/4*2 + 1/4*1)$ $= 6/20 + 1/20 + 16/20 = 23/20$. We can probably round up to 1.2 as a few people own more than 2 phones. That is 1 personal phone + 0.2 corporate phones.
> - Segment 3: we assume they would own 1 phone.
>
> The average replacement rate is equal to 1 on the phone lifespan. I suspect the lifespan is closer to 2 years for corporate phones whereas personal phones are replaced after about 4 years: (1 personal phone $*1/4$ + 0.2 corporate phone$*1/2$)/1.2= $(5/20 + 2/20)/1.2 = (7/20)/1.2 = 0.35/1.2$
>
> Regarding share, iPhones tend to be more expensive and very challenged by Android phones. However, the brand is very strong in the US so I would assume 2 phones out of 5 are an iPhone. Do these assumptions make sense?

Make assumptions based on your personal experience.

Fill-in your table as you make assumptions and calculate.

Use fractions where possible, as it makes calculations easier.

| SEGMENTS | OVERARCHING EQUATION | | | | |
| | UNIT OF ANALYSIS | x METRIC PER UNIT OF ANALYSIS | | | = |
	Number of people	Number of phones	Replacement rate	iPhone Share	Number of iPhones replaced
1) Teenagers/ students, 10-25 yo	60m	5/6	1/4	2/5	
2) Professionals, 25-60 yo	105m	1.2	0.35/1.2	2/5	
3) People not working or retired, 25-75 yo	95m	1	1/4	2/5	

We'll see. How many phones does this represent?

Let's calculate the number of iPhones replaced for each segment

| SEGMENTS | OVERARCHING EQUATION | | | | |
| | UNIT OF ANALYSIS | x METRIC PER UNIT OF ANALYSIS | | | = |
	Number of people	Number of phones	Replacement rate	iPhone Share	No. of iPhones replaced
1) Teenagers/ students, 10-25 yo	60m	5/6	1/4	2/5	**5m**
2) Professionals, 25-60 yo	105m	1.2	0.35/1.2	2/5	**~15m**
3) People not working or retired, 25-75 yo	95m	1	1/4	2/5	**9.5m**

Wrap-up calculations

Sense-check orders of magnitude

This gives us a total of about 30m iphones sold every year. That's equivalent to one American out of 10 or 11 purchasing an iPhone in a given year. It does not sound too unrealistic to me, maybe a bit low though.

This is indeed probably a bit on the low end. How would you refine this if you had more time?

Not having the perfect result is fine. Challenge your assumptions and think of ways to refine them in real life.

I know some people change iPhones every year, so I would try to refine the replacement rate to account for different behaviours. Similarly, more sophisticated segments may lead to very different market shares.

Agreed. Thank you for your time.

"IMPROVE UNDERSTANDING" BLOCKS
TROUBLESHOOTING

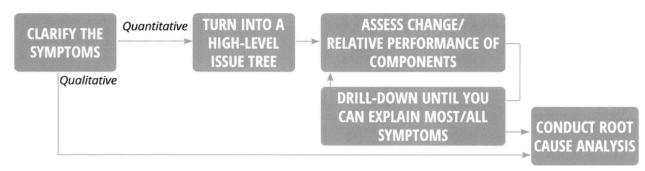

You will need to **troubleshoot when you hear about something not performing as expected**. These performance issues are usually the **surfacing symptoms** (e.g. revenue or profit drop, reputation, etc.). Troubleshooting aims at **pinpointing the areas in the business that malfunction**, before analyzing the **underlying root causes** (which can be very complex, internal and/or external).

You will also need to **understand whether you are solving for an industry or company problem, or both**.

1. CLARIFY THE SYMPTOMS

Quantify the problem as much as possible, **and define the relevant metrics**. Try as well to gather **context on the extent and history of the problem**.

- **Quantitative problem, e.g. "Profit dropped":**
  — Does this apply to the whole company or specific BUs/brand/products/geographies?
  — By how much has profit dropped, over which time frame? What is the absolute value and what was the previous value?
    > Then head to step 2 to drill-down.

- **Qualitative problem, e.g. "Corporate culture is problematic":**
  — What are the symptoms and implications? E.g. disengagement, churn, inappropriate behaviors, negative reputation, complaints and litigations, etc.
    ▪ Detail each symptom: e.g. disengagement could appear as an increase in absences, decrease in productivity, attitude...
  — How frequent are they? When has this started? What has been the financial performance in that period?
  — Clarify as well if this applies to the whole company or specific populations.
    > Then head directly to step 5 to brainstorm root causes.

2. TURN INTO A HIGH-LEVEL ISSUE TREE

Break down the components of the problematic performance metric(s) with an issue tree.
Whenever possible, use an equation, e.g. 30% of reduction of the net income translates into:

 Net Income = (Revenue – Op. Costs) – Depreciation/Amortization – Interests – Taxes

3. ASSESS CHANGE/RELATIVE PERFORMANCE OF COMPONENTS

Revenue drop?	Op. Costs increase?	D&A increase?	Interests Increase?	Taxes Increase?
-20%	+10%	-5%	+1%	-60%

Ask the interviewer **how these components have evolved,** and identify **those contributing most to the problem** (revenue drop and operational costs increase in the example above).

Ask as well if this is a **problem specific to the client company or impacting the whole sector.**

4. DRILL-DOWN UNTIL YOU CAN EXPLAIN MOST/ALL SYMPTOMS

Pick each of these problematic components and repeat the process, detailing the underlying components (e.g. here revenue = number of customers * number of items * item price).

- In a profitability problem, **pick revenue before costs** as costs can depend on revenue.

How many drill-down levels? The short answer is: **only a few** i.e. 1-3 — absolutely less than 5.

- **You need to assess all components at a given level before breaking down again** (see **pyramid principle**). If there are multiple components at a given level, you won't be able to drill-down many times in the limited time available in an interview.

- Conversely, if at each level there are not many components and only one is problematic, then you have the option to drill-down more — function of the time available in the case.

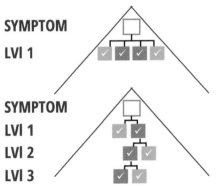

5. CONDUCT ROOT CAUSE ANALYSIS

Once problematic components have been identified, you should **look for root cause(s).**
For BU problems, leverage the **Ecosystem Map**, choosing the **right entry point** (see below).
For corporate problems, leverage **choices** outlined **in Corporate Strategy** (page 108).
Once root causes are identified, you can address them (see Achieve Target page 170).

• Regulations/ Governments	• Customers	• Value Chain / Suppliers/Partners	• Operating Model
• Trends	• Value propositions	• Level of Service	— Assets Model
			— Org. & Ways of working
			• Other/Culture

"IMPROVE UNDERSTANDING" BLOCKS
TROUBLESHOOTING EXAMPLE (1/3)

INTERVIEWER   **CANDIDATE**

Our client owns a daycare network in Sydney, Australia. Its profit has been plummeting for the past two years while he has been opening new centers around the city. He does not understand what is going on and we would like you to help him.

That sounds interesting! By how much has profit declined in the last 2 years? Also are we talking about the EBITDA, EBIT or net income?

Clarify the symptoms.

EBITDA has dropped 8% over a 2 year period.

Do we know how many centers our client owns? Is this trend affecting all the centers?

When your client operates different centers or stores or geographies, assess whether it is a problem across the board or for a subset only.

Good question. Our client owns 10 centers but this negative trend only affects the historic one, which is the biggest one with 120 kids spots.

Thank you. EBITDA = Revenue – Operating Costs so to troubleshoot our client's problem we will need to see if the issue is coming from revenue, costs, or both.

How have EBITDA and Revenue evolved in the past 2 years in this specific center?

Turn into a high-level issue tree.

Assess change/relative performance.

Revenue dropped 20% and EBITDA dropped 25%.

Interesting. This means we have both a revenue and cost issue impacting this center.

Let's deep-dive into the revenue drop first.

I don't have kids and I am not familiar with the Australian system but I would assume that a day care center generates revenue through the fees paid by families, plus potentially some additional private or public grants and subsidies, and additional elective services e.g. catering, nappies supply, extra-curricular activities.

Does this make sense or am I missing anything important in the Australian context?

The daily fee is paid by families but partly subsidized by the government for low-to-medium income families. There is no extra governmental subsidy for centers. Private donations are rare. Daily fees are high, around AUD 150, but generally include catering and nappies. Extra-curricular activities charged at a premium are actually very rare.

Drill-down by breaking the revenue component into a new equation.

Repeat the process and assess change/relative performance.

Alright so the main source of business to focus on can be broken down as: Revenue = number of kids * average number of days of attendance * average daily fee.

Have any of these components gone down in the past 2 years? If so, by how much and did other day care centers in a comparable area experience the same decline?

The average number of days of attendance has been stable. The average daily fee increased in line with the inflation. The number of kids dropped at our client's center though.

There are not many components in the equation and only one is problematic. The candidate thus decides here to go one level down before moving to costs.

Interesting. A drop in the number of kids could be driven by:

- A reduction in our capacity
- An exit rate above the historical average and/or
- A slower time to enroll new kids.

Has any of these happened?

"IMPROVE UNDERSTANDING" BLOCKS
TROUBLESHOOTING EXAMPLE (2/3)

An increase in the exit rate. What could explain this?

Good question. However, before we try to understand the root causes of this exit rate, can I just check whether this explains the 20% revenue drop of the center?

We also need to troubleshoot the incremental costs increase that removed another 5 EBIT percentage points...

We have identified the problematic factor for revenue. At this stage we could move to costs to explain the remainder of the EBIT drop. However, the interviewer enquires about the root cause. We follow his lead but remember to come back to costs later.

Good call. Yes the revenue drop is due to people withdrawing their kids. What about costs then?

Let's first list the center costs:
- Staff (educators, management and potentially cleaning, facility management, and kitchen)
- Real estate/building property or rent
- Utilities
- Other operating costs (audits, etc.)
- Marketing, if any.

What is your estimate of the relative importance of these cost buckets?

It is a care business, and it is located in a large city, so my rough guess would be that staff represents maybe 40%, real estate or rent another 30% and the remaining 30% would encompass the other costs (utilities, other operating costs and marketing).

Is that directionally correct?
Do we know which ones have gone up?

Directionnally yes. Staff costs have increased. Any idea why?

As for the revenue, we must understand which components of the cost base could explain the profit drop.

Let's break down the staff costs:

- Staff costs = number of FTEs * average salary per FTE.

If staff costs have increased, it means that:

- Either the number of FTE has increased.
- And/or there was an increase in average salary per FTE.

The average salary per FTE has increased. What could explain this?

Root cause analysis: the problem seems to be internal. Investigate an operating model or cultural problem (see page 152).

Note: if the staff had not left, it would be solely a revenue problem, in which case we would have started enquiring about new and more compelling value propositions for parents (e.g. a brand new center opening nearby, with lower fees).

OK. So parents withdrew their kids and staff left. It looks like something went wrong in the center. Let's try to understand the root causes.

Has anything changed in terms of people or assets, for instance a key person causing a problem, or major damages or risks in the center?

Actually, the center director left and a new director was appointed, but he was way too junior for the role. This led to a major disruption in the management and quality of care provided. The last satisfaction survey filled-in by parents was appalling and many withdrew their kids.

I see. Is this also the reason why staff left?

"IMPROVE UNDERSTANDING" BLOCKS
TROUBLESHOOTING EXAMPLE (3/3)

Yes. They had to be replaced with more expensive casual staff.
What would you recommend at this stage to our client?

We aim to restore profitability in the center.

There are several ways to achieve this. For instance, we could:

- Optimize the center in its current set-up, filling vacancies and if need be increasing price and/or reducing costs.
- Aim to restore the original value proposition.

I believe the former is probably not sustainable so I would focus on the latter and aim to reach full capacity, reduce kids' and staff's churn, restoring the original value proposition and communicating it to parents.

To do this, my advice would be to find within our client's network a high performing Director that could take a temporary assignment to turn around this center. This person should strive to:

- Engage with parents and staff to come up with solutions to problems shared in feedback surveys.
- Motivate the staff and retain them.
- Hire a new Director with the adequate experience to make the turnaround sustainable.

It is probably less critical but there might also be an opportunity to provide elective premium services to differentiate the center and marginally increase profitability.

Once you have troubleshot the problem, you are moving to an Achieve Target solving block to help the client.

This starts by defining your target, before listing and assessing options.

In an interview after a troubleshooting case you probably will not have a lot of time to think through options.

Focus on making a reasonable recommendation and outline concrete next steps.

"IMPROVE UNDERSTANDING" BLOCKS
MARKET DYNAMICS (E.G. INDUSTRY PROFILE)

Evaluating **market dynamics** fundamentally means:

- **Describing** the market and its dynamics **in a clear and concise way.**
- **Explaining** these dynamics, identifying **underlying drivers and trends.**

To do this, you need to look at all the **components of the Ecosystem Map**.

If your case study is solely a market dynamics case, you can **follow the structure outlined here** (there are many alternative frameworks but this one is quite easy to communicate).

When this block is **part of an Achieve Target problem** (see page 170), **focus only on the buckets helping you assess your options,** e.g.:

- **High-level analysis:** market performance when comparing markets.
- **Lower-level analysis:** customers, offers, and players when launching a new offering.

1. MARKET SCOPE AND PERFORMANCE

MARKET DEFINITION	• How do we define the boundaries of this market?
MARKET SIZE	• What is the market size? — Primarily in value — If relevant in volume.
MARKET GROWTH	• What are the growth dynamics? — E.g. "yo-yo" over the past few years, steady decline… — Comparing value vs. volume growth can help identify a change in average spend per customer (e.g. "premium-ization" or commoditization).
UNDERLYING DRIVERS & CURRENT TRENDS	• At the macro level – beyond the eco-system –, e.g. global economy downturn. • At the ecosystem level, e.g. cyclical long-term capacity-based industry, where people invest due to short-term opportunity leading to fast growth followed by excess capacities (such as LNG terminals).

2. CUSTOMERS AND OFFERS

CUSTOMERS
- What are the key customer segments?
- What are their key features and value drivers?
- Which proportion of the market size do they represent?

OFFERINGS
- Which types of value propositions exist in the market and what is their relative market share for each customer segment?
  - Note: identify as well substitutes not accounted for in the market size but meeting the customer needs.

3. PLAYERS

VALUE CHAIN
- Value chain for each type of value proposition (prioritized by relative importance in the market)
- Key steps in the value chain

MARKET STRUCTURE
- Level of fragmentation
- Key players along the value chain, for each value proposition:

Player 1

Player 2

Player 3

- Sources of competitive advantage (Key Success Factors) for leading players.

4. FUTURE

REGULATORY
- Regulatory changes or uncertainties

FUTURE TRENDS AND INNOVATION
- Trends expected to impact the industry:
  - Macro-trends
  - Industry trends (e.g. new operating models or new technology).

TOMORROW VS. TODAY
- Summary of potential impacts on the market performance, offers and market structure.

"IMPROVE UNDERSTANDING" BLOCKS
MARKET DYNAMICS EXAMPLE (1/3)

INTERVIEWER

CANDIDATE

> A steelmaker is considering increasing its capacity but wants to confirm first the demand potential in industrial sectors it did not target to date. They asked us to provide a perspective on the shipbuilding industry.

It is rare to have a case focused only on market dynamics. You will usually face these when asked about the potential or opportunity of a new geography or customer segment.

> Great! Let me just reframe to confirm I understood correctly the ask: our client wants to understand whether the shipbuilding industry could represent in the long run a demand for steel significant enough to justify investing into extra production capacity.
>
> Is that right?

Market dynamics assessment can be endless. Take the time upfront to clarify what the analysis is aiming to solve for to be more focused and relevant.

> That's right. They are also interested in the sustainability of that demand. How would you approach this?

Outline your approach.

> I suggest we first agree on the scope we are talking about and describe its size, dynamics and underlying drivers at a high-level.
>
> I would then deep-dive into customer needs and shipbuilders' offerings, as well as the market structure.
>
> Lastly I would like to understand the key trends or risks that may impact this industry. As we cover these, we can think about the implications for our steel manufacturer client. How does it sound?

> That sounds good.
> What would you like to know?

I would start with a few scoping questions:

1. What is the relevant geography for our market analysis? To keep things simple, I would advise we focus on areas where our client can actually export steel to.
2. How broad do we define shipbuilding? Is it only shipyards or do we include other stakeholders in the value chain (such as container manufacturers)? Also do we focus on building new boats or do we include the full lifecycle, with maintenance and ship breaking, which may have some impact on the demand for steel?
3. Last but not least, am I right assuming the client mandated us this year?

Don't assume the business problem takes place in the current year. Firms sometimes ask problems from decades ago to test your ability to solve without being helped by your knowledge of the current environment.

In this example, the problem is pre-COVID. You could ask whether to answer in a pre- or post-COVID world.

The project was commissioned at the beginning of 2019. Our client is based in Vietnam and primarily supplies the domestic construction sector. They are considering supplying steel to domestic shipyards only as neighbor maritime countries are already very prominent steelmakers.

At this stage we can neglect the impact of maintenance and steel scrapping. Vietnam shipyards are lagging behind in this space despite new laws enacted in 2014.

We can easily find online high-level data on the market size and trends so let's skip this.

I would actually like to hear your thoughts on the potential underlying drivers of the demand for new boats that you would analyze if you were in a project team.

The candidate needs to hear the steer from the interviewer and adapt the approach.

Well, I feel we need to go one level down and think about the different types of customers and ships, as drivers likely differ. For instance, I can think of:

- The shipping industry, buying containerships or cargo ships
- The fishing industry, buying trawlers
- The cruise industry, buying cruise ships
- Leisure boats like yachts and motor boats.

Am I missing any key customer or boat segments? Which ones are the most important for Vietnamese shipyards?

In a simple industry, you can start listing underlying drivers at a high level. For complex ones where there are very different customer segments, evaluate underlying drivers at the customer segment or value offering level.

"IMPROVE UNDERSTANDING" BLOCKS
MARKET DYNAMICS EXAMPLE (2/3)

There are actually many more segments, for instance:

On the private side you are missing bulk carriers, oil tankers, LNG and LPG carriers, ferry boats, scientific vessels, etc.

On the public side, military ships such as frigates, submarines, aircraft carriers, coastal patrol boats, etc.

However the picture is much simpler here: Vietnam shipyards historically focus on bulk carriers and mid-size containerships. In the past decade, Vietnam entered into the military space, building a few ships for their own army and securing a few international contracts but this remains marginal.

What could drive the building of new containerships and bulk carrier boats?

Containerships and bulk carriers are built to ship goods so we are first looking at the drivers of maritime trade level – the demand – before looking at the actual ship building – the offer –. Assuming shipyards can build ships for any country in the world, we can break down the trade level as:

Global Maritime trade level = global trade level * proportion of maritime trade vs. other routes

- The level of global trade is driven by the global economic growth as well as the incentives to trade internationally rather than producing locally e.g. difference in production costs between countries, border tariffs and export controls.
- The share of maritime vs. air vs. road is driven by the transportation cost, which is a factor of the distance between production and consumption and to some extent the cost of fuel.

Is this what you are looking for?

Validate that you are on track.

Yes. What about the shipbuilding dynamics?

Moving on to the offer, the number of new ships can be broken down as:

Global number of new ships * Vietnamese shipyards market share = total new ship capacity built/average ship capacity * Vietnamese shipyards market share.

- Let's focus on the new ship capacity built. The level of utilization of ships drives their profitability. This means that in an ideal world, demand should equal transport capacity. If demand exceeds available capacity, there is a capacity gap that will lead to new ships being built. This capacity gap is primarily driven by the trade growth we just mentioned.
- Also, ships need to be replaced after some time when they get too old. This can be evaluated by comparing the average age of the fleet with the average lifespan of those boats.
- I also heard about shipping companies replacing their fleet by brand new ships able to consume less fuel. This is a more opportunistic capacity replacement.
- Lastly, regulators may make some ships obsolete e.g. for environmental reasons.

To sum up:

New capacity built = capacity gap + normal capacity replacement + opportunistic capacity replacement + forced capacity replacement.

To get to the actual number of ships we can divide this new capacity by the average ship capacity. It may evolve, driven by technological advancements, but may also be limited by shipyards size constraints.

Does that make sense?

"IMPROVE UNDERSTANDING" BLOCKS
MARKET DYNAMICS EXAMPLE (3/3)

Yes. Beyond the growth, what should you look at when evaluating the capacity gap?

Well, if I make a parallel with other capex-intensive industries, I know there is often a delay in the capacity curve compared to the demand curve, due to the time required to build the capacity. This leads to cycles of under-capacity and high prices, followed by capacity gluts and drops in prices.

It would be interesting to know how significant this is in the shipbuilding industry as our client is interested in a sustainable demand.

Makes sense. What about the Vietnamese share?

It we will be a result of 3 interdependent factors, driving their level of competitiveness globally:

1. The quality of their production
2. Their price and
3. Their time to deliver boats.

The quality will depend on their local capabilities and the quality of their supply.

The price will depend on their cost base (supplies and labor), their profit margin vs. competition and the level of potential public subsidies.

Their delivery time will be impacted by their resource pool, work hours policies and access to key supplies such as steel.

Very good. A lot to look into for such a simple client ask, isn't it?

"IMPROVE UNDERSTANDING" BLOCKS
OTHER ENTITY (E.G. DUE DILIGENCE)

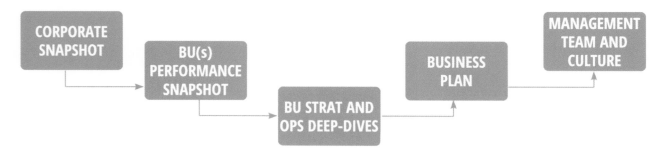

To differentiate the value proposition and make strategic choices, it is key to **understand key competitors.** To do this, we **profile** them, once again looking at the different parts of the **Ecosystem Map**, but **from their perspective** this time.

The steps below are usually followed in **M&A/due diligence projects.** The main challenge in these projects is to find the information, especially when the company is not listed. Calls with experts or former employees are usually the most effective tactic. You will thus probably **need this solving block in an Achieve Target problem** (see page 170), when the option to **partner with or acquire another entity** is considered.

Note that **in a case study,** you will probably only be able to **cover each of these buckets superficially. Focus on highlighting the key features, strengths and challenges/risks.**

1. CORPORATE SNAPSHOT

SHAREHOLDING PATTERN	• Who owns the company? — Public listed or private equity? — Majority owners and respective agenda/strategy?
PORTFOLIO	• Portfolio of activities and respective BU size — Revenue, EBIT(DA), headcount. • Offices/subsidiaries.
GOALS & ASPIRATION	• Corporate stated objectives

2. BU PERF. SNAPSHOT

MARKETS	• Geographies covered
PERFORMANCE	• Market share • Revenue & profit • Growth rate • Other relevant KPIs (e.g. safety ratio).

3. BU STRAT AND OPS DEEP-DIVES

VALUE OFFERINGS
- Target customers
- Value propositions and customer satisfaction.

VALUE CHAIN
- Roles(s) in the value chain
- Direct competitors.

OPERATING MODEL AND COMPETITIVE ADVANTAGES
- How do they operate?
  — Level of service vs. competitors
  — Key assets models choices (in-house vs. outsourced, geographic footprint, etc. see page 92)
  — Org. structure.
- Sources of competitive advantage (if any) i.e. what ultimately drives higher profit for them, e.g.:
  — Cost leadership: is their performance driven by the ability to deliver in a cheaper way than the rest of the market, thanks to scale, knowledge, technology...
  — Differentiation: do they bring unique and high-value offerings to the market?
  — Established barriers: have they secured part of the market by putting in place barriers to avoid new entrants coming in or preventing customers from switching from them (e.g. technology integration or long-standing relationships)?
  — Critical capabilities.
- Estimated cost structure.

4. BUSINESS PLAN

P&L
- Key growth and cost assumptions
- Forecast P&L (incl. cost of debt).

5. MANAGEMENT TEAM AND CULTURE

MUST-KNOW INFO
- Influential Executives?
- Culture reputation?
- Past issues suggesting potential risks (e.g. litigations, customer complaints, product recalls...)?

"ACHIEVE TARGET" APPROACH OVERVIEW

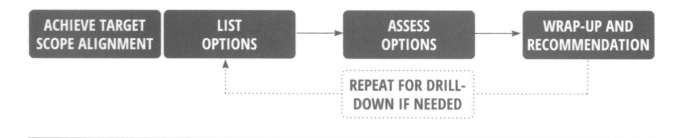

1. ACHIEVE TARGET SCOPE ALIGNMENT

After the first few minutes, you should have an initial sense of the client's need. If you identified it is an **ACHIEVE TARGET** case, you need to **formally align on the scope**, answering these questions:

1. **How do we define success**? What is the quantifiable metric(s) that defines a successful outcome?
2. **Are there key design principles or constraints** to factor-in (e.g. no change to staff, 25% opex reduction, recommendation should be applicable across all geographies...)?
3. **How will we compare options and decide** (e.g. strategic alignment, sales growth, EBIT, reputation, risk...)? **What is the relative importance of these criteria** (e.g. EBIT takes priority over revenue)?

2. LIST OPTIONS

Once the scope is defined, the most important step is to clearly list options to be compared:

*   **Limited number of MECE options (2 to 5)**
    *   If you come up with more than 5 you are probably listing options at a too granular level. Try to group them at a higher level, acknowledging there are variations.
*   **Framed as company choices (under the control of the company)**
*   **The option to do nothing should always be considered.** It is your baseline for reference and may be more profitable than any other moves.

Listing options is one of the hardest things to do and requires a good grasp of the business concepts outlined in previous chapters. A few things to keep in mind though:

*   **You are not expected to come-up with the perfect set of options.** You should propose something to refine and validate with the interviewer
*   **It is very hard to list options about a market you hardly know.** You can **start with a MARKET DYNAMICS block to first understand the market**, before listing options:
    *   E.g. "I would like first to understand a bit more who are the key customer groups and needs in this market, before listing a few options for our product launch".

YOU WILL FIND TIPS TO LIST OPTIONS IN FOLLOWING PAGES (SEE PAGE 172).

3. ASSESS OPTIONS

Lay out in a table your options and the key decision criteria for each.

It is now time to think about the best way to rate each option against each criterion. There is **no rule** so feel free to **pick first the option that seems easier**.

You **may need** to use one or several IMPROVE UNDERSTANDING **blocks** at this stage, to:

- Better understand customers, offers, competitors, ecosystem dynamics.

- Size something.

- Understand another entity (e.g. an M&A target, or a potential partner).

MARKET DYNAMICS

SIZING

OTHER ENTITY

4. WRAP-UP AND RECOMMENDATION

1. **Recap briefly the problem statement** (what is our client solving for?).
2. **State the recommended option, and why vs. others** (leveraging the decision criteria)
   — Note: you will rarely have an obvious answer, as there are pro's and con's for every option. Having defined at the beginning which criteria were more important than others should help pick a recommended option.
3. **Caveat recommendation** with any data gap, strong hypotheses used or risk factor.
4. State what **next steps** could look like (e.g. fill data gaps, get senior management onboard, look at options to implement the recommendations, etc.).

> REPEAT FOR DRILL-DOWN
> IF NEEDED

The process we have outlined in these pages may seem daunting and extremely long. In reality, it can be very quick if the problem is simple, options are straightforward and you do not need to conduct extensive deep-dives to assess options against decision criteria (e.g. you ask and the interviewer gives you the answer).

You may actually proactively build-in a "repeat loop" in your approach, to limit the level of complexity upfront, and focus the conversation.

E.g. "How to grow in Mexico?":

——————— ACHIEVE TARGET NO.1 ———————

1. WHERE TO GROW?

     ❯ EXPAND ROLE ON THE → 2. NEXT LEVEL DOWN   —— ACHIEVE TARGET NO.2 ——
        VALUE CHAIN

           ❯ ENTER RETAIL SPACE ——→ 3. HOW TO EXECUTE?

                             ❯ JV WITH FACILITY
                             MANAGEMENT COMPANY

"ACHIEVE TARGET"
HOW TO LIST OPTIONS? (1/3)

Here are a few shortcuts that can guide you to list options in an ACHIEVE TARGET case.
These are not silver bullets and you must tailor the logic and options to your specific problem.

We can usually distinguish 3 categories of ACHIEVE TARGET problems:

"SHOULD WE...?"

"HOW TO GROW/
IMPROVE/OPTIMIZE...?"

"HOW TO PRACTICALLY
SEIZE THE OPPORTUNITY/
LAUNCH/IMPLEMENT...?"

Reframe as "What would need to be true for this to be a good idea?", using Step 1 decision-making criteria.

Some cases are not that binary, and you need to list options on a continuum, e.g. "No" – "Yes to some extent" – "Yes".

The key here is to **list options at the relevant level** – see below –, which you should have identified at the beginning of the case.
With that in mind, you can **leverage** the key options outlined on the following pages.

This path implies that **the opportunity or project of interest is well defined already.**
If this is the case, you should start by clarifying which of the options below are on the table, before getting into more practical considerations — see page 176.
If this is not the case, consider options on the left.

A	COUNTRY / STATE LEVEL

A	YES

B	CORPORATE/MULTI-SECTORS LEVEL

B	YES TO SOME EXTENT

C	SECTOR / INDUSTRY / ECOSYSTEM LEVEL

A	ORGANIC GROWTH

B	MERGER & ACQUISITION (M&A)

C	NO

D	BUSINESS-UNIT / PRODUCT

C	JOINT-VENTURE (JV) / ALLIANCE

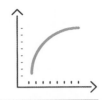

"HOW TO GROW/IMPROVE/OPTIMIZE...?"

A COUNTRY/STATE LEVEL   *See page 98*

Assuming the problem is related to internal affairs (not diplomacy or conflicts), consider the regulators' and governments' roles as potential options:

REGULATE

Regulate market structure & competitive dynamics?

Regulate customer needs or value offerings?

Regulate the level of service & operating models?

PLAY AN ACTIVE ROLE

Providing a public service (civil servants or via commissioning/delegation)?

Fostering ecosystems (investment, subsidies, PPP, etc.)?

B CORPORATE/MULTI-SECTORS LEVEL

Unless it is clear that the problem is limited to one SBS/BU (if so, you can leverage the guidance outlined on the next page), assess whether any of these higher-level corporate choices could be relevant options:

Adjust the portfolio of activities?

 See page 112

Adjust the org. structure?

 See page 114

Adjust the financial strategy?

 See page 110

C SECTOR/INDUSTRY/ECOSYSTEM LEVEL

If the client is an industry association or consortium, think about its potential roles, e.g.:

Conduct joint industry promotion?

Provide services to members (e.g. special deals)?

Lobby with regulators/governments?

Setting & controlling standards or legislating for their sector.

Set-up alliances/joint initiatives, e.g. integrated supply chain.

"ACHIEVE TARGET"
HOW TO LIST OPTIONS? (2/3)

"HOW TO GROW /IMPROVE/OPTIMIZE...?" (CONTINUED)

D BUSINESS-UNIT / PRODUCT

If the focus of the problem is on the top line ("How to/where to grow?"), assess whether multiple strategic growth options are plausible (see below).

If yes, start with these and **narrow down** with the interviewer if they are on the table for the client. If multiple options are indeed on the table, it probably makes sense to stay at that strategic level, before getting more granular.

If not, i.e. if the problem turns out to be quite focused and **only one strategic option is relevant** (check with the interviewer), then **go one level down** in the issue tree.

E.g. "How to price a **new range** of products?" would probably be a deep-dive into the strategic growth option number 2 (adjacent offering).

TOP LINE ⟶ STRATEGIC GROWTH OPTIONS

1 GROW CURRENT MARKET AND/OR OFFERING	**3** EXPAND ROLE ON THE VALUE CHAIN
2 EXTEND REACH OF CURRENT OFFERING OR INTRODUCE ADJACENT OFFERING	**4** ENTER SIGNIFICANTLY DIFFERENT MARKET

If the focus of the problem is on the bottom line (e.g. "How to improve EBIT?"), conduct first a troubleshooting to see if there are improvement opportunities or issues to deal with at the top line level (customers, competitors, value proposition, role), before looking at internal factors.

TROUBLESHOOT ⟶ KEY INTERNAL DECISIONS

TOP LINE OPPORTUNITIES

If there are top line opportunities, follow steps outlined above.

BOTTOM LINE FOCUS ONLY

Otherwise, assess whether any of the key internal decisions are on the table, before doing a deep-dive.

A REVISIT ROLE ON THE VALUE CHAIN AND/OR PARTNERS
B ADJUST LEVEL OF SERVICE
C CHANGE THE ASSETS MODELS
D ADJUST ORG. STRUCTURE & WAYS OF WORKING

TOP LINE OPTIONS – NEXT LEVEL DOWN

1 First narrow down the list of relevant in-market growth drivers (see page 66).

*You can use a **customer journey (p72)** or **buying process (p73)** to identify the tangible opportunities in front of relevant drivers and to assess them.*

2 Narrow down geographies first to limit complexity, then deep-dive in each to identify a set of alternative and meaningful segments x value proposition.

Assess options leveraging Achieve Target Step 1 decision criteria to prioritize opportunities.
*You may for instance need to **segment (p74)** the market and/or assess customers' **willingness to pay (p85)**.*

3 Map the value chain and identify steps capturing most of the value (opportunity to expand).

*Assess Step 1. decision criteria for each step of interest. Consider the size of the financial opportunity and the risks/barriers — see **opportunity prioritization framework (p75)**.*

4 Approach 1: list strategic capabilities and use cases e.g. in other industries.

Approach 2: list customer pain points and brainstorm solutions.

*Approach 1: identify company most **value-adding steps (p88)**.*

*Approach 2: **customer journey (p72)**.*

BOTTOM LINE OPTIONS – NEXT LEVEL DOWN

A Same as Option 3 above, but with a focus on problematic/costly steps. Consider renegotiating partnerships, expanding on the value chain or conversely refocusing.

B Identify key business processes first (either problematic or most resource intensive). Then list alternative level of service (speed – quality – flexibility) tradeoffs — see page 88.

C Focus on problematic or resource intensive processes and define alternative RoA tradeoffs (level – effectiveness – cost) — see page 90.

D Focus on problematic or most resource intensive processes and improve the org. structure and ways of working — see page 94.

NB: keep in mind that making a change internally might impact the value proposition, hence the top line, and eventually the EBIT(DA).

"ACHIEVE TARGET"
HOW TO LIST OPTIONS? (3/3)

"HOW TO PRACTICALLY SEIZE THE OPPORTUNITY/LAUNCH/IMPLEMENT...?"
E.g. How to establish a presence in the high-end jewelry
market in Tier 1 cities in China?

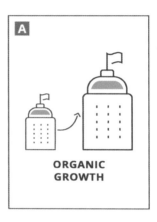

A

ORGANIC GROWTH

B

MERGER & ACQUISITION (M&A)

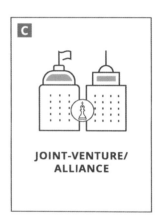

C

JOINT-VENTURE/ ALLIANCE

To decide between these options, we need to **consider**:

- **The role(s) on the value chain and the level of service needed:**
  — To deliver the value proposition.
  — To communicate the value proposition.
  — To make the value proposition accessible.

- The **capabilities and scale** required to deliver that level of service.
- The **financial, risk and speed impacts** of building these capabilities ourselves vs. "leapfrogging" with inorganic growth, noting that:
  — Mergers and acquisitions may be limited by antitrust laws; they may as well induce significant purchase and integration costs.
  — Alliances mean sharing the intellectual property and the value generated.

- The likely **competitive response.**

"ACHIEVE TARGET"
EXAMPLE (1/3)

INTERVIEWER   CANDIDATE

INTERVIEWER: You inherit a vineyard in the Bordeaux area. What do you decide to do with it?

CANDIDATE: That's interesting! Do we have a bit more info on this vineyard and what success should look like for me?

Align on the problem scope before diving into the resolution.

INTERVIEWER: Sure. It is a small vineyard producing Bordeaux wines that are mainly sold overseas. The vineyard is a bit old-fashioned but is still compliant with all the regulations in place.

In terms of success, it is up to you to define it, but it appears you have a EUR 5m debt to repay within the next 10 years, following a former unsuccessful venture.

EUR 5m debt is a key constraint.

CANDIDATE: Oh, it means I really need to generate cash one way or another through this vineyard!

Do I still have any investment capacity (equity or debt)? Also, do I have any experience in the wine industry or is this new to me?

INTERVIEWER: Yes you can still borrow debt as long as you demonstrate a robust business case allowing to cover for your previous debt repayments and the new ones.

You have some exposure to the wine industry via your family but you have not operated a vineyard yourself.

The ability to borrow debt is a key design principle (it broadens the range of options on the table).

Limited experience is a key constraint.

CANDIDATE: Alright, so my goal is to at least pay back this debt and hopefully make some more money. What I propose is that we list a few distinct strategic options and then assess them, looking at the:

- Total profit generated
- Ability to repay debt on time
- Likelihood of success/risk.

Definition of success.

Overarching Achieve Target approach.

Criteria to compare options. In this example the ability to repay the former debt on time is the main criterion helping to prioritize options.

INTERVIEWER: Seems sensible. Where do you start?

I can think of 3 fairly distinct approaches:

1. On one end of the spectrum, I could sell the vineyard today and finish this venture
2. Somehow in-between, I could maintain the status quo, operate the vineyard as it is and keep the current cash flows.
3. On the other end of the spectrum, I could invest time, effort and cash to grow the business and generate positive cash flows to repay my debt and hopefully earn money. There are probably many variations to this scenario.

3 valid options. There are indeed alternative ones, but for the sake of time, let's stick to these.

OK then let's focus first on option 1:

- The total profit generated would be a one-off cash flow equivalent to the selling price after all fees, minus taxes. In addition I need to consider the profit or loss from operations until the vineyard is sold.
- My ability to repay debt will thus depend on the total profit above and the time needed to sell the property, which depends on the attractiveness of my land, assets and business, relative to similar vineyards in the region.
- The level of risk should be relatively low compared to other options as I do not need to rely on running a new business to generate cash. It is the easiest option.

Do we have a sense of the potential selling price and the attractiveness of my vineyard for potential buyers?

How would you define the selling price?

I would try to triangulate the selling price with different valuation methods:

- Asset-based: looking at the sum of the value of the assets
- Cash-flow based: calculating the expected cash flows to define its net present value.
- Comparator-based: looking at other similar vineyards recently sold in the area.

Have we done these valuations already?

"ACHIEVE TARGET"
EXAMPLE (2/3)

Yes. The land is actually quite valuable so you could generate about EUR 5m from the sale, taxed at 30%. You are likely to wait 18 to 24 months to find a buyer and close the deal. What is the expected profit from this option?

We said earlier that my total profit will be the sum of a) the sale after tax and b) the profit or loss from operations in the next say 24 months.

For a) it is pretty simple: EUR 5m*70%= EUR 3.5 m.

Let's evaluate b). Do we have a P&L to leverage?

In short, revenue amount to about EUR 8m per year. Sales are not increasing, largely due to very active competition overseas.

Gross Margin is 15%. Yearly Opex amount to EUR 900k and there are no recurring investments. Some machinery needs to be replaced, costing about EUR 300k, depreciated over 3 years.

Gross profit is 15% of 8m = 1.2m... minus 900k Opex, this gives us 300k in EBITDA.The new machinery will remove 100k per year for 3 years. That gives a 200k EBIT, minus 30% tax equals EUR 140k in net income per year for 2 years. To summarize for option 1:

- I will get about 3.5m + 0.14*2m=3.78m within 2 years.
- This represents only 75% of my total debt, but I have 8 more years to repay the remainder. If I invested the money and got a moderate financial return (e.g. 5%), I could probably repay it in full.
- The level of risk is low compared to other options.

It is overall a relatively good option. Shall we move to option 2?

Sure

Option 2 is the status quo i.e. operating the vineyard as it is now. We calculated already the profit for the next 2 years.

Do we expect the financials to be similar in the following 8 years, assuming nothing changes?

It is probably directionally correct overall, with some highs and lows.

Then this means we generate 140k income for 3 years, while we depreciate the new machinery. In following years, the EBIT will be EUR 100k higher i.e. 300k. Minus 30% tax rate... net income equals 210k. After 10 years, I will have earned 140k * 3 + 210k * 7 = 1.89m.

This is much lower than Option 1. To sum up:

- I cannot repay my debt with these cash flows.
- It is not even a guaranteed income as we may face climatic hazards disrupting operations from times to times.

I will discard this option and evaluate Option 3.

Agreed

The question with Option 3 is the following: can we make the vineyard significantly more profitable with targeted investments (acknowledging I can borrow more with a strong business case).

As EBIT = revenue minus costs, I will first look into top line growth opportunities and then evaluate the impact on the bottom line.

What are your ideas to increase revenue?

This is a "HOW TO" question at a BU/small business level, with a TOP LINE focus, nested under the higher level options.

See Where to Grow page 66.

Conceptually, I can think of 4 main ways:

1. Grow our current market, increasing the number of customers and/or the average basket price.
2. Extend our reach (new segments, geographies, channels) and/or our range of grape-based beverages (alcoholic or non-alcoholic).
3. Move down the value chain, for instance by capturing value in the wholesale, retail or even transport steps as we sell overseas.
4. Expand into another market, e.g. hospitality, weddings and functions.

Which of these are on or off the table?

"ACHIEVE TARGET"
EXAMPLE (3/3)

That's a good list. 3 is definitely a stretch. 4 may be feasible but will not be a significant source of business. You could consider expanding your customer base for your wine, but you are unlikely to develop new products in the short term.

OK. Before doing any detailed analyses of markets, segments and needs, I would like to understand the theoretical maximum revenue I could generate with my wine production.

The revenue of the vineyard corresponds to the sale of wine bottles: Revenue = number of bottles sold * average wholesale price.

- On volume: can we produce and sell more bottles, considering our grapes production and processing capacity?
- On price: do we have an opportunity to increase our selling price, through differentiation or by changing distribution channels?

You could produce 50% more bottles. RE prices, you rely on international wholesalers and represent a small volume, so you are unlikely to meaningfully increase prices.

Right. So my annual revenue could theoretically grow by 50% i.e. up to $12m if I manage to sell these incremental bottles. Do we have a sense of the potential demand for my wines?

Prices would increase over that time horizon with inflation, but we ignore this factor to simplify the problem and to be on the conservative side.

Your parents didn't invest at all in marketing efforts. The website is very old school and it appears there is an opportunity to grow the B2C market easily, without large investments.

A preliminary analysis estimates a +20% increase in sales next year, followed by +5% YoY, with a yearly EUR 100k marketing investment.

That seems a great move. Are there any cost-saving opportunities in addition?

Some machines could be upgraded this year to increase productivity of the wine production. It would cost 600kEUR on top of the mandatory investments. However, it would provide a 10 percentage point gross margin uplift from next year onwards. How does it sound?

It sounds good. Let's see how the P&L evolves with these assumptions:

	Year 1	Year 2	Year 3	Year 4	Year 5	Year 6	Yrs 7--10
Revenue	8m	9.6m (+20%)	~10.1m (+5%)	~10.6m (+5%)	~11.1m (+5%)	~11.7m (+5%)	12m (prod. cap)
Gross Margin %	15%	25%	25%	25%	25%	25%	25%
Gross Profit	1.2m	2.4m	~2.525m	~2.650m	~2.775m	~2.925m	3m
- Opex	– 900k	– 900k	– 900k	– 900k	– 900k	– 900k	– 900k
- Mktg Opex	– 100k	– 100k	– 100k	– 100k	– 100k	– 100k	– 100k
EBITDA	200k	1.4m	~1.525m	~1.650m	~1.775m	~1.925m	2m
- Replacements	– 100k	– 100k	– 100k	/	/	/	/
- Upgrades	– 200k	– 200k	– 200k	/	/	/	/
EBIT	– 100k	1.1m	~1.225m	~1.650m	~1.775m	~1.925m	2m
- Tax @30%	/	~ – 330k	~ – 370k	~ – 500k	~ – 530k	~ – 580k	600k
Net income	– 100k	770k	855k	1.15m	1.245m	1.345m	1.4m
Cumulative	– 100k	670k	1.525k	2.675m	3.920m	5.265m	6.665m

Even though I am making a loss in year 1, this if offset in year 2. I am able to repay my debt by year 6 and generate more than 1m a year afterwards, when I have reached my production cap. To summarize:

- This option is the most attractive financially speaking.
- It allows to repay the debt in full before the 10-year deadline.
- It is at the same time the most risky option:
  — It requires investments.
  — It heavily relies on strong revenue upside and productivity improvement assumptions.
  — It does not factor-in any climatic hazard impacting production.
  — It is a new business for me.

What is your recommendation at this stage?

Wrap-up and recommendation. Suggest concrete next steps.

My recommendation at this stage would be to deep-dive into Option 3 to make the case more robust, for instance:

- Assess whether there is an opportunity to raise prices if I now focus on the B2C market.
- Confirm the productivity gains are actually feasible and allowed by industry standards.
- Seek to mitigate upfront some of the risks (e.g. onboarding experienced people, securing long term supply agreements with wholesales, etc.).
- Evaluate the business opportunity of the side businesses we mentioned.

Anyhow, if the business case remains uncertain I would take Option 1 as a fallback plan.

That being said, as you mentioned earlier, the land is the valuable part of the vineyard. I would also like to evaluate alternative options, e.g. remove the vineyard, lease the land, build another more profitable business on the land...

PRACTICAL TIPS
CHEAT SHEET – STARTING THE CASE

1. LISTEN AND TAKE NOTES
Listen to the interviewer and capture the client's ask and data points.

IN PARALLEL, THINK ABOUT THE
PROBLEM YOU ARE ASKED TO SOLVE

2. THEN CLARIFY THE SCOPE

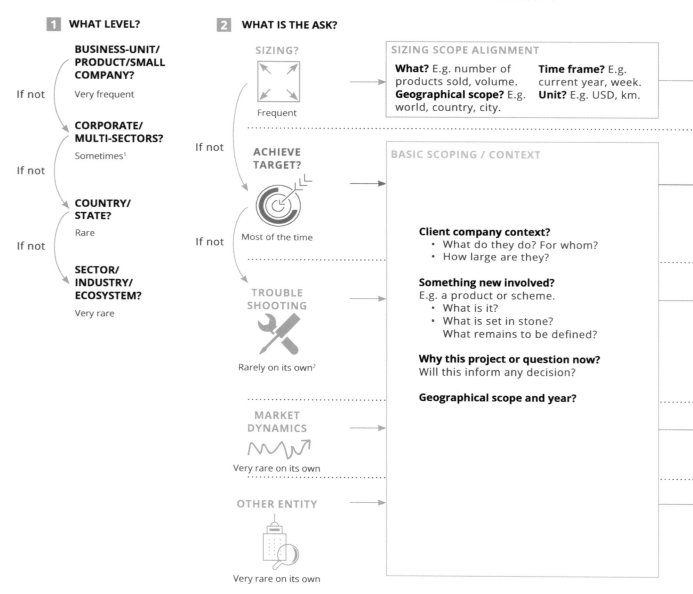

1 WHAT LEVEL?

BUSINESS-UNIT/ PRODUCT/SMALL COMPANY?
Very frequent

If not

CORPORATE/ MULTI-SECTORS?
Sometimes[1]

If not

COUNTRY/ STATE?
Rare

If not

SECTOR/ INDUSTRY/ ECOSYSTEM?
Very rare

2 WHAT IS THE ASK?

SIZING?

Frequent

If not

ACHIEVE TARGET?

Most of the time

If not

TROUBLE SHOOTING

Rarely on its own[2]

MARKET DYNAMICS

Very rare on its own

OTHER ENTITY

Very rare on its own

SIZING SCOPE ALIGNMENT

What? E.g. number of products sold, volume.
Geographical scope? E.g. world, country, city.
Time frame? E.g. current year, week.
Unit? E.g. USD, km.

BASIC SCOPING / CONTEXT

Client company context?
- What do they do? For whom?
- How large are they?

Something new involved?
E.g. a product or scheme.
- What is it?
- What is set in stone? What remains to be defined?

Why this project or question now?
Will this inform any decision?

Geographical scope and year?

---

1. It is very rare that interviewers explicitly mention that the client is a corporate/multi-sectoral group. In doubt, double check.

2. Case studies are very often framed as a troubleshooting ("this problem happened, why?"). However, it is very rare to try and troubleshoot an issue without trying to fix it (becoming an ACHIEVE TARGET problem). Clarify with the interviewer what the client's aspiration (or challenge) is once you have troubleshot the problem.

3. OUTLINE THE APPROACH, VALIDATE WITH THE INTERVIEWER AND START SOLVING

see page 140

see page 170

see page 152

see page 160

see page 168

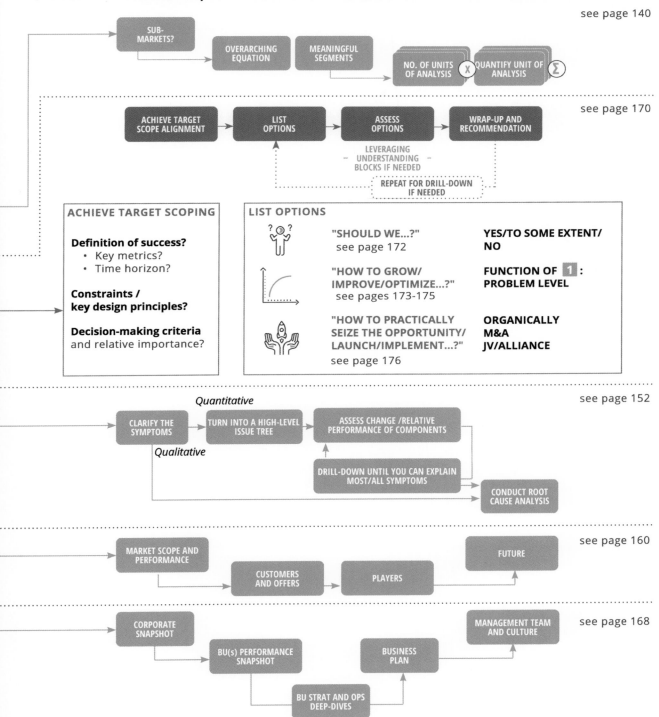

SUB-MARKETS?

OVERARCHING EQUATION

MEANINGFUL SEGMENTS

NO. OF UNITS OF ANALYSIS (X) QUANTIFY UNIT OF ANALYSIS (Σ)

ACHIEVE TARGET SCOPE ALIGNMENT → LIST OPTIONS → ASSESS OPTIONS → WRAP-UP AND RECOMMENDATION

LEVERAGING UNDERSTANDING BLOCKS IF NEEDED

REPEAT FOR DRILL-DOWN IF NEEDED

ACHIEVE TARGET SCOPING

Definition of success?
- Key metrics?
- Time horizon?

Constraints / key design principles?

Decision-making criteria and relative importance?

LIST OPTIONS

"SHOULD WE...?"
see page 172

"HOW TO GROW/ IMPROVE/OPTIMIZE...?"
see pages 173-175

"HOW TO PRACTICALLY SEIZE THE OPPORTUNITY/ LAUNCH/IMPLEMENT...?"
see page 176

YES/TO SOME EXTENT/ NO

FUNCTION OF **1** : PROBLEM LEVEL

ORGANICALLY M&A JV/ALLIANCE

Quantitative

CLARIFY THE SYMPTOMS → TURN INTO A HIGH-LEVEL ISSUE TREE → ASSESS CHANGE /RELATIVE PERFORMANCE OF COMPONENTS

Qualitative

DRILL-DOWN UNTIL YOU CAN EXPLAIN MOST/ALL SYMPTOMS

CONDUCT ROOT CAUSE ANALYSIS

MARKET SCOPE AND PERFORMANCE

CUSTOMERS AND OFFERS

PLAYERS

FUTURE

CORPORATE SNAPSHOT

BU(s) PERFORMANCE SNAPSHOT

BU STRAT AND OPS DEEP-DIVES

BUSINESS PLAN

MANAGEMENT TEAM AND CULTURE

PRACTICAL TIPS
NOTE TAKING

Interviewers can request to keep your notes at the end of the interview, for confidentiality reasons or to see how you take notes.

Bring a few sheets of paper, a pencil and eraser to take notes during your case (cleaner than using a pen and crossing out).

Structure your notes on different pages to organize the different types of information.

One page with the information the interviewer shared with you at the beginning of the interview (e.g. background, experience, expertise) and the answers to your questions at the end of the interview (fit part).

You can keep this page if we take your notes.

We advise you to put the name of the interviewer and consulting firm on top of the pages to be able to classify the different interviews you went through.

One case overview page, where you capture the case study statement, the basic scoping information and your overarching approach.

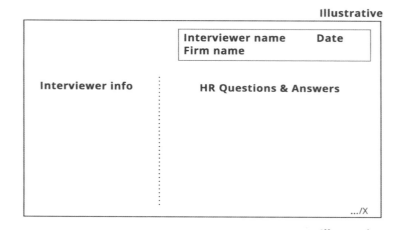

If you ideate options using a framework (an issue tree, a buying process...), **cross-out options discarded and highlight those selected.**

Clearly **identify** the main **assumptions** and **results** you are reaching (e.g. by drawing a box around them).

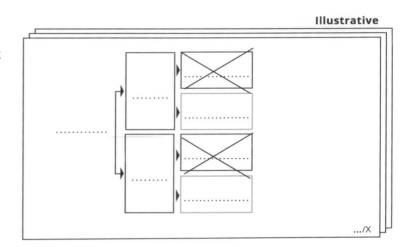

Try to have a **dedicated page to capture your key insights/results (and key assumptions)** as you progress.

If this is an **Achieve Target case,** you should **put together upfront a table with the options assessed and the decision-making criteria.**

You may also capture on the side potential **next steps**.

It will, combined with the case overview page, allow you to **wrap-up** the case.

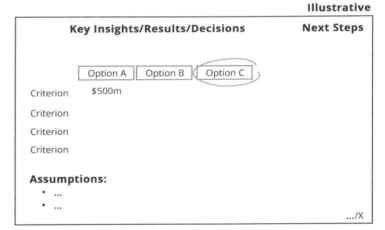

A few extra tips:

- **Write down detailed calculations on separate pages** to avoid messy pages.
- Do not hesitate to **draw** things (on a blank page).
- Make sure you can **easily navigate** through your notes (e.g. to check a previous data point):
  — Write on **one side** only.
  — Use **HEADINGS** to quickly identify what you are reading.
  — If you use many pages, **number** them.

Note: these are only tips based on our experience. Feel free to take notes differently as long as you are comfortable and able to effectively navigate through these.

PRACTICAL TIPS
SLIDE 101

PowerPoint slides are consultants' primary way to convey and support messages to clients.

The interviewer may ask you to **sketch a slide** during a case study, to see how you would visualize and communicate your insights.

How to write a slide:

- A good slide is **simple** to understand: not crowded and straight to the point.
- Each slide should have an **insightful** (rather than descriptive) "action title".
  Note: ideally, slide titles should align with the executive summary (see page 35).

Slides will often include a **chart** or table:

- It should have its own short **title** and include **scope, units and data time frame**.
- Charts also include an easy-to-read **legend**.

In addition, the slide can include **insightful bullet points** to help the reader **interpret** the data.

Data **sources or references** should always be stated in the slide footer.

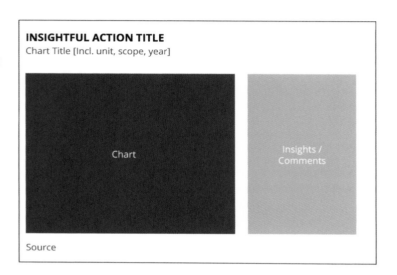

See below illustrative examples of charts you need to be familiar with.
Consultants use an Office add-on, called Thinkcell, to easily build these.

BAR CHART

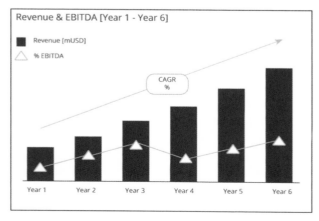

WATERFALL CHART

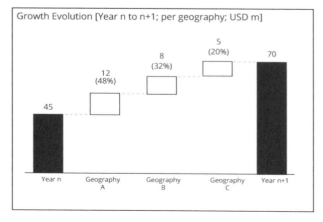

WATERFALL/PARETO CHART

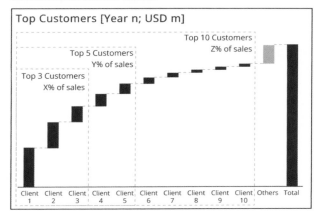

LINE CHART

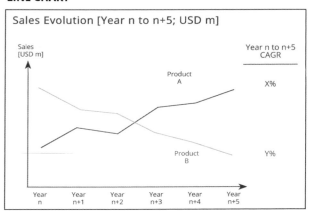

SCATTER (2 VARIABLES)/BUBBLE CHART (3 VARIABLES)

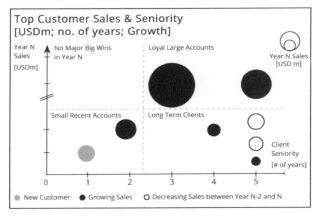

HARVEY BALLS CHART (QUALITATIVE ASSESSMENT)

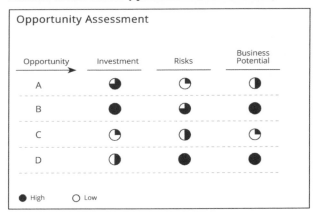

COMPARATIVE CHART (QUALITATIVE ASSESSMENT)

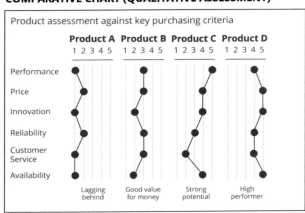

MARIMEKKO

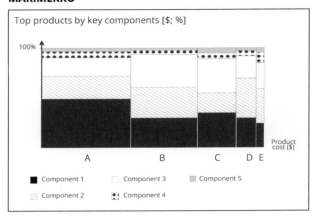

PRACTICE & IMPROVE

TEST YOUR PROBLEM-SOLVING APPROACH

- Test your problem-solving skills with the attached **dry runs** (see page 194).
- Review the **general orders of magnitude** provided (see page 211) and prepare your **local orders of magnitude** for sizing exercises (see page 220).

THEN PRACTICE WITH 10-20 MOCK INTERVIEWS

WITH FRIENDS/PEERS

Focus on the identification of the case type to get more and more familiar with the Solving Blocks methods.

WITH EXPERIENCED CONSULTANTS (AT LEAST 50%)

Focus on the scoping and structured case resolution and practice wrapping-up the case.

Free ——————— Who to practice with? ————————→ $$$

ALUMNI   **ONLINE PLATFORM**   **COACH**

REFLECT ON EACH CASE STUDY COMPLETED

- After each practice case, **document the case** and how you approached it (see template below).
- Then, it is very important that you take the time to **revisit the solving approach and steps**, and identify how you could do better with a similar problem in the future.

 TEMPLATE

	○	**INTERVIEWER**
	CASE TRACKING	
PROBLEM STATEMENT		**DATE**
• ...		
THE APPROACH I FOLLOWED		
• ...		
HOW TO SOLVE THIS TYPE OF CASES NEXT TIME?		

CASE TYPE	• ...	**POTENTIAL BLOCK SEQUENCE**	• ... • ... • ...
INITIAL RESPONSE	• ... • ... • ...	**KEY STEPS**	• ... • ... • ...

STRATINTERVIEWS

PRACTICE CASE STUDIES IN A NEAR-REAL ENVIRONMENT

MAXIMIZING COMPETENCE AND CONFIDENCE

COVERING BOTH ESSENTIAL & ADVANCED BUSINESS CASES (MBA)

HOW DOES IT WORK?

1

LISTEN TO THE INTERVIEWER & ANSWER IN REAL TIME

Your time to answer is limited, replicating the pressure experienced during interviews.

2

PLAY-BACK THE VIDEO & ANSWER SELF-ASSESSMENT QUESTIONS

Put yourself in the interviewer's shoes and immediately identify elements to work on.

3

REVIEW WHAT GOOD LOOKS LIKE

Listen to a top candidate's answer and review the metholodology and case-specific tips, before moving on to the next step.

4

IDENTIFY YOUR DEVELOPMENT AREAS

Listen to a top candidate's answer and review the metholodology and case-specific tips, before moving on to the next step.

Practice mock interviews on www.stratinterviews.com

HOMEWORK

CASE
DRY RUNS

CASE STUDY DRY RUNS

For each business case below:

1. **Identify the case type (level & client ask).**
2. **Derive the potential block sequence.**
3. **Write below how you would respond to the interviewer in the first few minutes.**
4. **Outline the steps you might follow afterwards.**

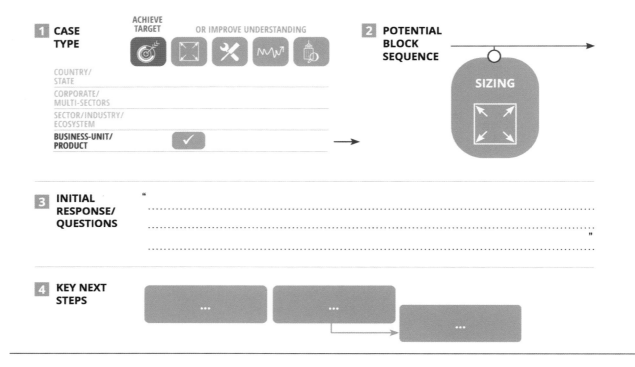

1	**GEOMETRIC ESTIMATE**	What is the height of the Empire State Building?
2	**REVENUE/MARKET ESTIMATE**	What is the global revenue of McDonald's?
3	**BU REVENUE GROWTH CURRENT MARKET**	A Telco challenger wants to aggressively capture market share from the incumbent. What would you do?
4	**BU REVENUE GROWTH ALL OPTIONS**	A frozen fried producer wants to grow their revenue. How would you help them?

5 PRICING A NEW PRODUCT

A Japanese consumer electronics player is planning to launch its brand new digital gigapixel camera and would like to know how to price it.

6 RESTORE PROFITABILITY

The leading car rental company experienced last year a drop in EBIT. How could you help them?

7 OPERATIONAL REVIEW

Our client operates offshore oil platforms. Their security ratio significantly dropped in the past 2 quarters. What could explain this?

8 BREAKEVEN ANALYSIS

An electric battery manufacturer wants to understand whether producing a next-generation battery for electric vehicles would be profitable.

9 GO/NO GO

A large coffee shop brand is considering launching a royalty program. Should they do it?

10 COST REDUCTION/ PROCUREMENT REVIEW

A Canadian cookie manufacturer saw its profit drop due to increased costs. They want to restore it through a cost-reduction exercice. What should they focus on?

11 PRIVATE EQUITY/ MERGERS & ACQUISITIONS

The head of a PE fund asks us whether they should invest in a startup which has developed solar panel films that can be applied on any surface or window, and if so, how?

12 COMPETITIVE ADVANTAGE

The Chief Operations Officer of Boeing asked us to provide a summary of Airbus' competitive advantage in the long-haul plane segment.

13 POST-MERGER INTEGRATION

Two leading defence technology players announced their merger. The COE of Company A would like to define next steps to integrate with Company B.

CASE STUDY DRY RUNS – PROPOSED APPROACH

1 GEOMETRIC ESTIMATE

What is the height of the Empire State Building?

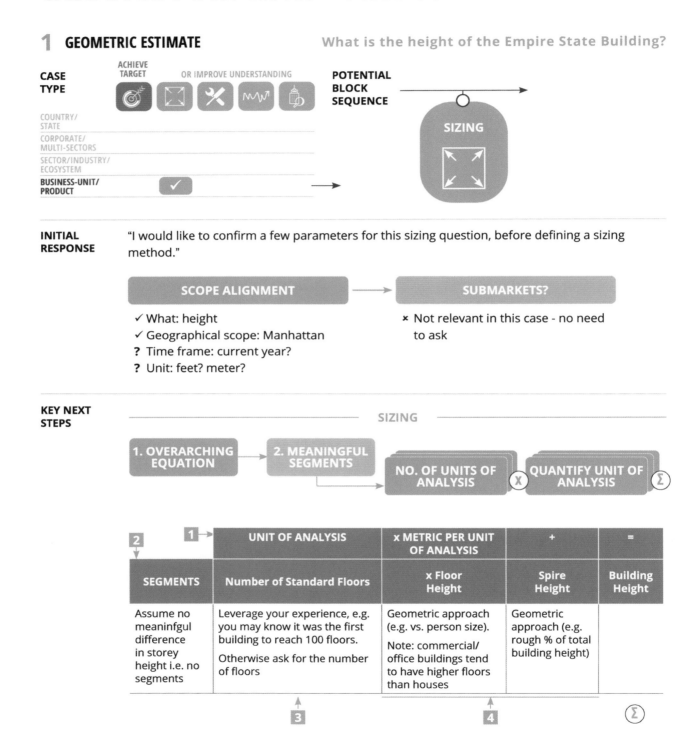

CASE TYPE

ACHIEVE TARGET   OR IMPROVE UNDERSTANDING

COUNTRY/STATE
CORPORATE/MULTI-SECTORS
SECTOR/INDUSTRY/ECOSYSTEM
BUSINESS-UNIT/PRODUCT ✓

POTENTIAL BLOCK SEQUENCE

SIZING

INITIAL RESPONSE

"I would like to confirm a few parameters for this sizing question, before defining a sizing method."

SCOPE ALIGNMENT

✓ What: height
✓ Geographical scope: Manhattan
? Time frame: current year?
? Unit: feet? meter?

SUBMARKETS?

✗ Not relevant in this case - no need to ask

KEY NEXT STEPS

SIZING

1. OVERARCHING EQUATION → 2. MEANINGFUL SEGMENTS → NO. OF UNITS OF ANALYSIS ⓧ QUANTIFY UNIT OF ANALYSIS Σ

	UNIT OF ANALYSIS	x METRIC PER UNIT OF ANALYSIS	+	=
SEGMENTS	**Number of Standard Floors**	**x Floor Height**	**Spire Height**	**Building Height**
Assume no meaninfgul difference in storey height i.e. no segments	Leverage your experience, e.g. you may know it was the first building to reach 100 floors. Otherwise ask for the number of floors	Geometric approach (e.g. vs. person size). Note: commercial/office buildings tend to have higher floors than houses	Geometric approach (e.g. rough % of total building height)	

2 REVENUE/MARKET ESTIMATE

What is the global revenue of McDonald's?

CASE TYPE

ACHIEVE TARGET   OR IMPROVE UNDERSTANDING

COUNTRY/STATE

CORPORATE/MULTI-SECTORS

SECTOR/INDUSTRY/ECOSYSTEM

BUSINESS-UNIT/PRODUCT ✓

POTENTIAL BLOCK SEQUENCE

SIZING

INITIAL RESPONSE

"I would like to clarify first a few scoping elements, before outlining a sizing approach."

SCOPE ALIGNMENT	SUBMARKETS?
? What: HQ rent & royalties or sum of franchisees' revenue?	? Operational revenue only (e.g. not financial revenue)
✓ Geographical scope: global	
? Time frame: current year?	
? Unit: USD?	

KEY NEXT STEPS

"Let's define our sizing equation and our relevant segments, before quantifying the revenue for each."

SIZING

1. OVERARCHING EQUATION → 2. MEANINGFUL SEGMENTS → 3. NO. OF UNITS OF ANALYSIS × 4. QUANTIFY UNIT OF ANALYSIS Σ

| SEGMENTS Country Archetypes based on pop. density & purchase power | UNIT OF ANALYSIS Number of Restaurants | × METRIC PER UNIT OF ANALYSIS: RESTAURANT ANNUAL REVENUE | | | = |
		× Daily Customers	× Average Basket Price	× No. Opening Days	Global Revenue
Archetype A	Pop. approach	Productive Approach (no. of checkouts)	Starting Assumption	Assumption	
Archetype B	Pop. approach		Assumption (leveraging Big Mac or PPP index)	Assumption	
...	Pop. approach		Assumption (leveraging Big Mac or PPP index)	Assumption	

CASE STUDY DRY RUNS – PROPOSED APPROACH

3 BU REVENUE GROWTH CURRENT MARKET

A Telco challenger wants to aggressively capture market share from the incumbent. What would you do?

CASE TYPE

ACHIEVE TARGET · OR IMPROVE UNDERSTANDING

COUNTRY/ STATE

CORPORATE/ MULTI-SECTORS — ?

SECTOR/INDUSTRY/ ECOSYSTEM

BUSINESS-UNIT/ PRODUCT — ?

HOW TO? >> GROW TOP LINE >> CURRENT MARKET →

POTENTIAL BLOCK SEQUENCE

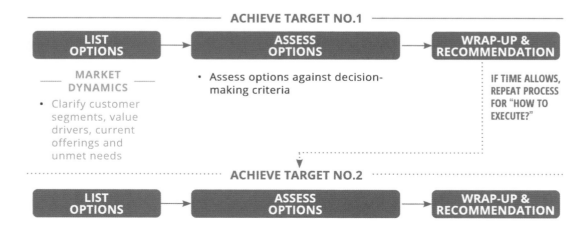

ACHIEVE TARGET NO.1 WHERE TO GET SHARE FROM?

ACHIEVE TARGET NO.2 HOW TO EXECUTE?

ACHIEVE TARGET · MARKET DYNAMICS · ACHIEVE TARGET

INITIAL RESPONSE

"I would like to clarify first the scope and our client's aspiration and goals."

BASIC SCOPING / CONTEXT	→	ACHIEVE TARGET SCOPING

BASIC SCOPING / CONTEXT
- **?** Company overview: how do we define the market and where do our client and the incumbent operate (internet, mobile, landline, TV, media/advertising, cloud/IT services...)?
- **?** Geographic footprint?
- **?** Why grow now?
- **?** Time frame for this case?

ACHIEVE TARGET SCOPING
- **?** Definition of success? Share of customers or in value? Target %?
- **?** Constraints/key principles? Time horizon? Room for maneuver?
- **?** Decision-making criteria and relative importance?
- **?** Strategic growth option: grow in current market (same customers and offerings)?

KEY NEXT STEPS

"I suggest we first deep-dive into the market dynamics to list and prioritise growth opportunities. I will then assess them against our client's goals and decision criteria to make a recommendation. If time allows, I would like to repeat this process to think about the options on the table to seize these growth opportunities."

──────── ACHIEVE TARGET NO.1 ────────

LIST OPTIONS	→	ASSESS OPTIONS	→	WRAP-UP & RECOMMENDATION

MARKET DYNAMICS
- Clarify customer segments, value drivers, current offerings and unmet needs

- Assess options against decision-making criteria

IF TIME ALLOWS, REPEAT PROCESS FOR "HOW TO EXECUTE?"

──────── ACHIEVE TARGET NO.2 ────────

LIST OPTIONS	→	ASSESS OPTIONS	→	WRAP-UP & RECOMMENDATION

4 BU REVENUE GROWTH ALL OPTIONS

A frozen fries producer wants to grow their revenue. How would you help them?

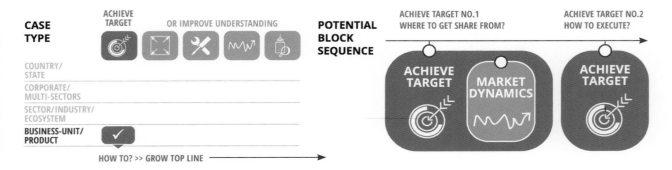

CASE TYPE

ACHIEVE TARGET | OR IMPROVE UNDERSTANDING

COUNTRY/STATE
CORPORATE/MULTI-SECTORS
SECTOR/INDUSTRY/ECOSYSTEM
BUSINESS-UNIT/PRODUCT ✓

HOW TO? >> GROW TOP LINE

POTENTIAL BLOCK SEQUENCE

ACHIEVE TARGET NO.1 WHERE TO GET SHARE FROM? — ACHIEVE TARGET NO.2 HOW TO EXECUTE?

ACHIEVE TARGET — MARKET DYNAMICS — ACHIEVE TARGET

INITIAL RESPONSE

"I have a few questions for you regarding the company context, and I would like then to frame a bit more with you this growth project, before diving into growth options."

BASIC SCOPING / CONTEXT	→	ACHIEVE TARGET SCOPING

BASIC SCOPING / CONTEXT
- **?** Company overview: footprint, customers, value proposition and role in the value chain? Current revenue/market share?
- **?** Why grow now?
- **?** Time frame for this case?

ACHIEVE TARGET SCOPING
- **?** Definition of success? Target growth?
- **?** Constraints/key principles? Time horizon? Room for maneuver?
- **?** Decision-making criteria and relative importance?

KEY NEXT STEPS

"I suggest we first list and prioritise *where to grow* opportunities, before repeating, if time allows, this process to select options to *seize* these prioritized growth opportunities. For the first part, we need to start by narrowing down the range of strategic moves on the table. Then, we will be able to deep-dive in the market dynamics to outline more concrete growth opportunities to assess against our clients goals and decision criteria."

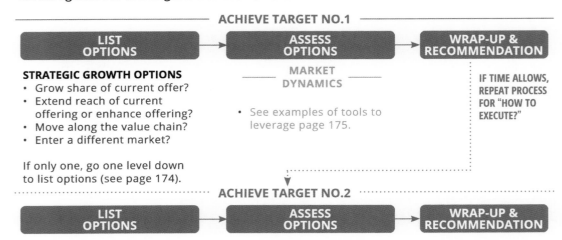

———————— ACHIEVE TARGET NO.1 ————————

LIST OPTIONS → **ASSESS OPTIONS** → **WRAP-UP & RECOMMENDATION**

STRATEGIC GROWTH OPTIONS
- Grow share of current offer?
- Extend reach of current offering or enhance offering?
- Move along the value chain?
- Enter a different market?

If only one, go one level down to list options (see page 174).

MARKET DYNAMICS
- See examples of tools to leverage page 175.

IF TIME ALLOWS, REPEAT PROCESS FOR "HOW TO EXECUTE?"

············ ACHIEVE TARGET NO.2 ············

LIST OPTIONS → **ASSESS OPTIONS** → **WRAP-UP & RECOMMENDATION**

CASE STUDY DRY RUNS – PROPOSED APPROACH

5 PRICING A NEW PRODUCT

A Japanese consumer electronics player is planning to launch its brand new digital gigapixel camera and would like to know how to price it.

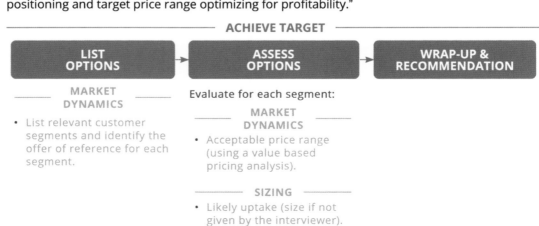

CASE TYPE

COUNTRY/STATE

CORPORATE/MULTI-SECTORS

SECTOR/INDUSTRY/ECOSYSTEM

BUSINESS-UNIT/PRODUCT ✓

HOW TO? >> GROW TOP LINE >> NEW OFFERING

POTENTIAL BLOCK SEQUENCE

ACHIEVE TARGET
WHICH SEGMENT * VALUE PROPOSITION, HENCE PRICE?

ACHIEVE TARGET — MARKET DYNAMICS — SIZING

INITIAL RESPONSE

"I would like to understand the key features of this new camera and the company's aspiration for this launch, before defining a pricing approach."

BASIC SCOPING / CONTEXT	ACHIEVE TARGET SCOPING
? Company overview: competitive positioning, size, footprint	**?** Definition of success?
? Key attributes of the new camera? How will it fit in the portfolio? COGS?	**?** Constraints/key principles? Time horizon? Pricing room for maneuver?
? Launch markets and timelines?	**?** Decision-making criteria and relative importance (e.g. revenue vs. EBIT, lack of cannibalization)?
? Price to be set — e.g. wholesaler or RRP?	

KEY NEXT STEPS

"We need to understand in our launch market(s) the set of alternative customer segments and positioning (hence price points) that are on the table. We will then be able to assess their attractiveness by conducting on one hand a value based pricing analysis, and on the other hand an estimation of the likely uptake. This price-volume analysis will help us define the final positioning and target price range optimizing for profitability."

ACHIEVE TARGET

LIST OPTIONS	ASSESS OPTIONS	WRAP-UP & RECOMMENDATION
MARKET DYNAMICS	Evaluate for each segment:	
• List relevant customer segments and identify the offer of reference for each segment.	MARKET DYNAMICS	
	• Acceptable price range (using a value based pricing analysis).	
	SIZING	
	• Likely uptake (size if not given by the interviewer).	

6 RESTORE PROFITABILITY

The leading car rental company experienced last year a drop in EBIT. How could you help them?

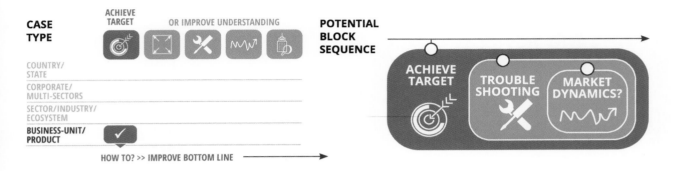

CASE TYPE

ACHIEVE TARGET — OR IMPROVE UNDERSTANDING

COUNTRY/STATE
CORPORATE/MULTI-SECTORS
SECTOR/INDUSTRY/ECOSYSTEM
BUSINESS-UNIT/PRODUCT ✓

HOW TO? >> IMPROVE BOTTOM LINE

POTENTIAL BLOCK SEQUENCE

ACHIEVE TARGET → TROUBLE SHOOTING → MARKET DYNAMICS?

INITIAL RESPONSE

"I would like to understand first a bit more the clients' context and what their ambition is. Then, we should troubleshoot the EBIT drop and understand the underlying root cause. With that, we will be able to think through options to improve the situation."

BASIC SCOPING / CONTEXT	→	ACHIEVE TARGET SCOPING

BASIC SCOPING / CONTEXT

? Company overview: geographic footprint, target customer segments and value propositions, key competitors

ACHIEVE TARGET SCOPING

? Definition of success? EBIT target rate? Time horizon?
? Constraints/key principles? Pricing room for maneuver?
? Decision-making criteria and relative importance (e.g. revenue vs. EBIT, speed, staff retention...)?

KEY NEXT STEPS

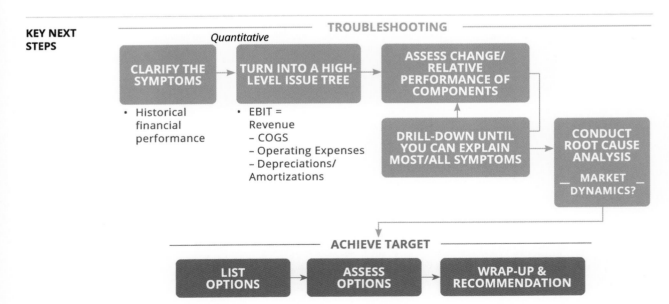

TROUBLESHOOTING

Quantitative

CLARIFY THE SYMPTOMS
• Historical financial performance

→ **TURN INTO A HIGH-LEVEL ISSUE TREE**
• EBIT = Revenue
  – COGS
  – Operating Expenses
  – Depreciations/ Amortizations

→ **ASSESS CHANGE/ RELATIVE PERFORMANCE OF COMPONENTS**

DRILL-DOWN UNTIL YOU CAN EXPLAIN MOST/ALL SYMPTOMS

CONDUCT ROOT CAUSE ANALYSIS
_ MARKET DYNAMICS? _

ACHIEVE TARGET

LIST OPTIONS → **ASSESS OPTIONS** → **WRAP-UP & RECOMMENDATION**

CASE STUDY DRY RUNS – PROPOSED APPROACH

7 OPERATIONAL REVIEW

Our client operates offshore oil platforms. Their security ratio has significantly dropped in the past 2 years. What could explain that?

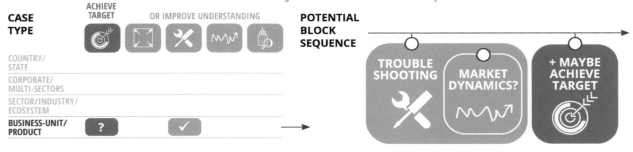

CASE TYPE

ACHIEVE TARGET — OR IMPROVE UNDERSTANDING

COUNTRY/STATE
CORPORATE/MULTI-SECTORS
SECTOR/INDUSTRY/ECOSYSTEM
BUSINESS-UNIT/PRODUCT — ? ✓

POTENTIAL BLOCK SEQUENCE

TROUBLE SHOOTING → MARKET DYNAMICS? → + MAYBE ACHIEVE TARGET

INITIAL RESPONSE

"I hear that our client wants us to primarily diagnose what is going wrong. To troubleshoot this problem, I would like to first clarify the context of this security ratio drop, to then drill-down and identify the key components or parameters that are responsible for this drop. Then I would like to try and understand the underlying root causes (either internal or external). If time allows, we can think about ways to resolve this issue."

BASIC SCOPING / CONTEXT

? Company overview: geographic footprint, role in the value chain (e.g. owning platforms? key suppliers?)

? How is the security ratio calculated and what are standard values and deviation

KEY NEXT STEPS

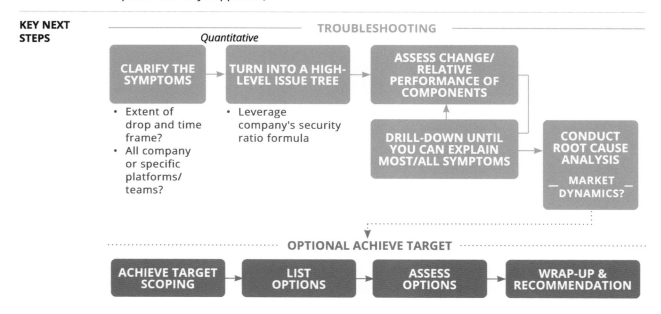

TROUBLESHOOTING

Quantitative

CLARIFY THE SYMPTOMS
- Extent of drop and time frame?
- All company or specific platforms/teams?

TURN INTO A HIGH-LEVEL ISSUE TREE
- Leverage company's security ratio formula

ASSESS CHANGE/RELATIVE PERFORMANCE OF COMPONENTS

DRILL-DOWN UNTIL YOU CAN EXPLAIN MOST/ALL SYMPTOMS

CONDUCT ROOT CAUSE ANALYSIS
— MARKET DYNAMICS?

OPTIONAL ACHIEVE TARGET

ACHIEVE TARGET SCOPING → **LIST OPTIONS** → **ASSESS OPTIONS** → **WRAP-UP & RECOMMENDATION**

8 BREAKEVEN ANALYSIS

An electric batttery manufacturer wants to understand whether producing a next-generation battery for electric vehicles would be profitable.

CASE TYPE

ACHIEVE TARGET   OR IMPROVE UNDERSTANDING

COUNTRY/STATE
CORPORATE/MULTI-SECTORS
SECTOR/INDUSTRY/ECOSYSTEM
BUSINESS-UNIT/PRODUCT ✓

SHOULD WE?

POTENTIAL BLOCK SEQUENCE

ACHIEVE TARGET → MARKET DYNAMICS → SIZING

INITIAL RESPONSE

"From a decision-making perspective, this is equivalent to asking: "what would need to be true for this to be profitable?". Many factors can impact the answer. Before proposing an approach, I would like to understand what this decision entails for the company, what is set and what the room for maneuver is. I also need to understand the company's aspiration."

BASIC SCOPING / CONTEXT	→	ACHIEVE TARGET SCOPING

BASIC SCOPING / CONTEXT

? Company overview: footprint, role in the value chain, customers and value proposition, competitive positioning, size
? Key attributes of the next generation battery, implications of producing it and knowns vs unknowns (e.g. target price, likely uptake)
? How would this next generation battery fit in the portfolio (replace current or complement)?

ACHIEVE TARGET SCOPING

? Definition of success?
? Constraints/key principles? Time horizon? Pricing room for maneuver?
? Decision-making criteria and relative importance (e.g. revenue vs. EBIT, lack of cannibalization)?

"With this framing set, let's list the key strategic options and let's assess each of them against the company's decision-making criteria to make a recommendation."

KEY NEXT STEPS

——————————————— ACHIEVE TARGET ———————————————

LIST OPTIONS E.G.	→	ASSESS OPTIONS	→	WRAP-UP & RECOMMENDATION

- Do not produce.
- Repurpose current production lines.
- Invest in additional production lines.
- ...

MARKET DYNAMICS

SIZING (IF NEEDED)

CASE STUDY DRY RUNS – PROPOSED APPROACH

9 GO/NO GO

A large coffee shop brand is considering launching a loyalty program. Should they do it?

CASE TYPE

ACHIEVE TARGET   OR IMPROVE UNDERSTANDING

COUNTRY/STATE
CORPORATE/MULTI-SECTORS
SECTOR/INDUSTRY/ECOSYSTEM
BUSINESS-UNIT/PRODUCT   ✓

SHOULD WE?

POTENTIAL BLOCK SEQUENCE

ACHIEVE TARGET → MARKET DYNAMICS → SIZING

INITIAL RESPONSE

"Answering whether a loyalty program should be put in place really depends on the nature of the loyalty program structure and the appetite for it. I thus would like to first understand what the company is trying to achieve, what has been decided already, and summarize the options on the table. We can then assess the business impact of each option and make a recommendation, leveraging the company's decision-making criteria."

BASIC SCOPING / CONTEXT	ACHIEVE TARGET SCOPING
? Company overview: footprint, role in the value chain, customers and value proposition, competitive positioning, size? **?** Key attributes of the loyalty program, knowns vs unknowns (e.g. design, value to customers, operating model and cost of running, expected impact on company's revenue...)? **?** Why launch this program now?	**?** Definition of success (e.g. revenue uptake) **?** Constraints/key principles? Time horizon? Room for maneuver? **?** Decision-making criteria and relative importance (profit, revenue, brand...)?

"With this framing set, let's list the key strategic options and let's assess each of them against the company's decision-making criteria to make a recommendation."

KEY NEXT STEPS

ACHIEVE TARGET

LIST OPTIONS E.G. → ASSESS OPTIONS → WRAP-UP & RECOMMENDATION

- Launch in-house program.
- Join a multi-sector loyalty program.
- Do nothing.
- ...

MARKET DYNAMICS

SIZING (IF NEEDED)

10 COST REDUCTION / PROCUREMENT REVIEW

A Canadian cookie manufacturer saw its profit drop due to increased costs. They want to restore it through a cost-reduction exercice. What should they focus on?

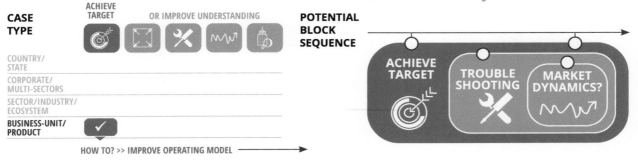

CASE TYPE

ACHIEVE TARGET   OR IMPROVE UNDERSTANDING

COUNTRY/ STATE

CORPORATE/ MULTI-SECTORS

SECTOR/INDUSTRY/ ECOSYSTEM

BUSINESS-UNIT/ PRODUCT ✓

HOW TO? >> IMPROVE OPERATING MODEL

POTENTIAL BLOCK SEQUENCE

ACHIEVE TARGET → TROUBLE SHOOTING → MARKET DYNAMICS?

INITIAL RESPONSE

"I would like to understand first the company's context and clarify what the aspiration is when it comes to restoring profitability. We will then troubleshoot the profit drop and aim to understand the underlying root causes. From there, we can think about options to restore the profitability, with a particular focus on cost-reduction."

BASIC SCOPING / CONTEXT	ACHIEVE TARGET SCOPING
? Company overview: footprint, role in the value chain, customers and value proposition, size?	**?** Definition of success (e.g. revenue uptake)
? Implications of the profit drop? What is at stake?	**?** Constraints/key principles? Time horizon? Room for maneuver?
	? Decision-making criteria and relative importance (profit, revenue, brand...)?

KEY NEXT STEPS

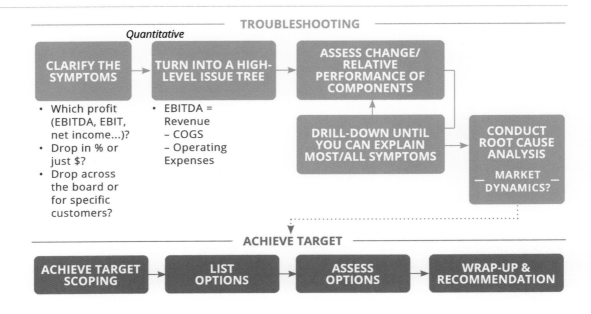

TROUBLESHOOTING

Quantitative

CLARIFY THE SYMPTOMS
- Which profit (EBITDA, EBIT, net income...)?
- Drop in % or just $?
- Drop across the board or for specific customers?

TURN INTO A HIGH-LEVEL ISSUE TREE
- EBITDA = Revenue – COGS – Operating Expenses

ASSESS CHANGE/ RELATIVE PERFORMANCE OF COMPONENTS

DRILL-DOWN UNTIL YOU CAN EXPLAIN MOST/ALL SYMPTOMS

CONDUCT ROOT CAUSE ANALYSIS
— MARKET DYNAMICS? —

ACHIEVE TARGET

ACHIEVE TARGET SCOPING → **LIST OPTIONS** → **ASSESS OPTIONS** → **WRAP-UP & RECOMMENDATION**

CASE STUDY DRY RUNS – PROPOSED APPROACH

11 COMPETITIVE ADVANTAGE   The Chief Operation Officer of Boeing asked us to provide a summary of Airbus' competitive advantage in the long-haul segment.

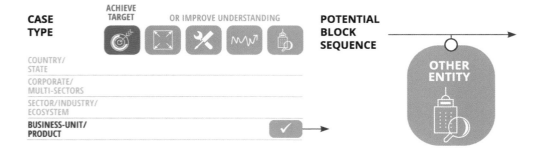

CASE TYPE

ACHIEVE TARGET · OR IMPROVE UNDERSTANDING

COUNTRY/ STATE
CORPORATE/ MULTI-SECTORS
SECTOR/INDUSTRY/ ECOSYSTEM
BUSINESS-UNIT/ PRODUCT ✓

POTENTIAL BLOCK SEQUENCE

OTHER ENTITY

INITIAL RESPONSE

"Before profiling Airbus in the long haul segment, I would like to understand briefly the context for the client request, to help focus the analysis."

BASIC SCOPING / CONTEXT

? Which decision is this client request supposed to inform? Are we trying to explain something in particular?

? What is the scope of the analysis (geographic scope, time frame, specific aircrafts or customers?)?

KEY NEXT STEPS

"Let's start the analysis by how the long-haul segment fits in the broader Airbus business and what its business performance has been, relative to our client or the rest of the industry. This will allow us to quantify the extent of their competitive advantage. We will then deep-dive into its strategy and operating model to try and identify its sources of competitive advantage. If time allows, I would also like to check how the management team and the organisation culture might contribute to the competitive advantage."

OTHER ENTITY

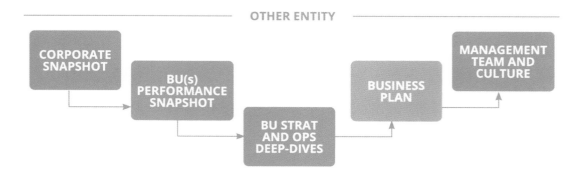

12 PRIVATE EQUITY/ MERGERS & ACQUISITIONS

The lead of PE fund X asks us whether they should invest in a startup which has developed solar panel films that can be applied on any surface or window, and if so how?

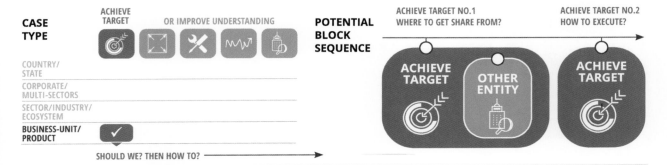

CASE TYPE

COUNTRY/STATE
CORPORATE/MULTI-SECTORS
SECTOR/INDUSTRY/ECOSYSTEM
BUSINESS-UNIT/PRODUCT ✓

SHOULD WE? THEN HOW TO?

INITIAL RESPONSE

"Let's align first on the fund's objectives, constraints and decision-making criteria. We can then translate these into a set of prerequisites for any investment and check if the target startup ticks all the boxes. If it does, we can then think about the right approach for the fund to invest (e.g. minority stake, majority stake, full acquisition via LBO, MBO, etc.)."

BASIC SCOPING / CONTEXT

? Fund overview: footprint, assets under management and key investors, industry focus, investment time frame?

? Target overview: is it for sale? Has it been valued already? Were due diligences (strategic, financial, legal, HR, etc.) commissioned already?

ACHIEVE TARGET SCOPING

? Definition of success? Target return and time frame?

? Constraints/key principles? Room for maneuver (e.g. cash in hand, access to debt, exits planned)?

? Decision-making criteria (turn into prerequisites for investment)?

KEY NEXT STEPS

"Let's check if the target startup meets the fund's prerequisites. I propose we first analyze the shareholding pattern and footprint, before looking at the different businesses the startup operates in, their performance, strategy and operating model. From there, I will try to estimate the potential business plan of the company over the next few years and eventually try to profile the management team and culture."

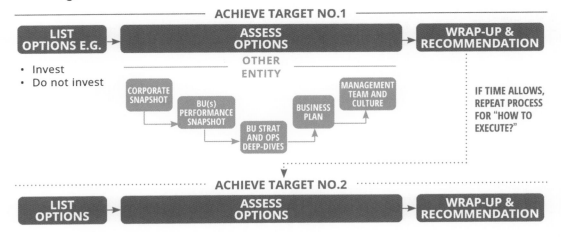

CASE STUDY DRY RUNS – PROPOSED APPROACH

13 POST-MERGER INTEGRATION (PMI)

Two leading defence technology players announced their merger. The CEO of Company 1 would like to define next steps to integrate with Company 2.

CASE TYPE

ACHIEVE TARGET | OR IMPROVE UNDERSTANDING

COUNTRY/STATE

CORPORATE/MULTI-SECTORS — 2 companies involved

SECTOR/INDUSTRY/ECOSYSTEM

BUSINESS-UNIT/PRODUCT

HOW TO? >> IMPROVE BOTTOM LINE (POTENTIALLY TOP LINE TOO)

POTENTIAL BLOCK SEQUENCE

INITIAL RESPONSE

"I would like to clarify first the context and scope of the merger, as well as the agenda of our client, the CEO of Company 1."

BASIC SCOPING / CONTEXT	ACHIEVE TARGET SCOPING
? Companies overview: relative size, role in the value chain (competing or complementing?) **?** Merger context: how advanced is the merger process, what is the governance (what about the other CEO?), what is the geographical scope?	**?** Definition of success for the merger for our client (Company 1 CEO)? **?** Constraints/key principles? Time horizon? Room for maneuver? **?** Decision-making criteria and relative importance (EBIT impact, culture, retention...)?

KEY NEXT STEPS

"I imagine at this stage there are a number of discrepancies and overlaps in the consolidated entity, either because pre-merger decisions have not yet been enforced, or because decisions remain to be made. I suggest we list these systematically at the corporate and BU level. This diagnosis may reveal the need to prioritize specific decisions or projects, in which case we can assess alternative roadmaps and recommend one, leveraging the CEO's decision criteria."

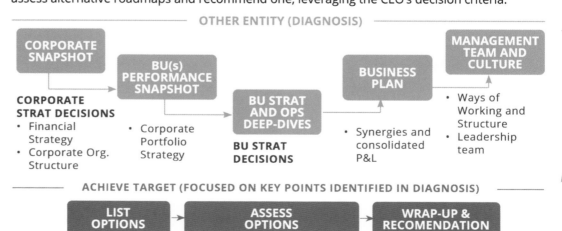

OTHER ENTITY (DIAGNOSIS)

CORPORATE SNAPSHOT

CORPORATE STRAT DECISIONS
• Financial Strategy
• Corporate Org. Structure

BU(s) PERFORMANCE SNAPSHOT
• Corporate Portfolio Strategy

BU STRAT AND OPS DEEP-DIVES

BU STRAT DECISIONS

BUSINESS PLAN
• Synergies and consolidated P&L

MANAGEMENT TEAM AND CULTURE
• Ways of Working and Structure
• Leadership team

ACHIEVE TARGET (FOCUSED ON KEY POINTS IDENTIFIED IN DIAGNOSIS)

LIST OPTIONS → ASSESS OPTIONS → WRAP-UP & RECOMENDATION

HOMEWORK

ORDERS OF
MAGNITUDE
FOR REALITY CHECKS

ORDERS OF MAGNITUDE
POPULATION REFERENCES

Having **orders of magnitude** in mind will help you **challenge and stress-test your own assumptions and results**. We listed in this section key data points helpful for sizing problems. The following list is not exhaustive but gives you an idea of what you should be familiar with.

Take the time to create your **personal reference sheet**, adapting these values for your **local market** (see template page 220).

1. TOTAL POPULATION

Population per Continent (2020)

Continent	Population (Bn)
World	7.80
Asia	4.64
Africa	1.34
Europe	0.75
Latin America and the Caribbean	0.65
Northern America	0.34
Oceania	0.04

Population of Main Countries (2020 – Sample)

Countries	Population (Millions)
China	1,439
India	1,380
USA	331
Brazil	213
Russian Federation	146
Mexico	129
Germany	84
UK	68
France	65
Canada	38

Population per Main Cities (2020 – Sample)

Megalopolis >10m inhabitants		Metropolis – Tier 1 Cities 1m to 10m inhabitants		Tier 2 100k to 1m inhabitants	Tier 3 Up to 100k inhabitants
Tokyo	37.4m	Seoul	9.9m		
Delhi	30.3m	London	9.3m		
Sao Paulo	22.0m	Chicago	8.9m		
Shanghai	27.1m	Hong Kong	7.5m		
Mexico City	21.8m	Santiago	6.7m	Look-up the list for your own country (check the source below). As a minimum, know roughly how many cities fit in each category and how many people live in each on average).	
Beijing	20.5m	Madrid	6.5m		
Mumbai	20.4m	Singapore	5.8m		
NYC	18.8m	Saint-Petersburg	5.4m		
Moscow	12.5m	Sydney	4.8m		
Paris	11.0m	Berlin	3.6m		

Source: UN Habitat – Global Database of Metropolises – 2020

2. DEMOGRAPHIC DATA

Average household size

- Approx. 3 in developed countries — average of families (4+), single people (1) and elderly (1 or 2)
- Average number of child per women: 2.5

Average people per age group

Iillustration in a developed country.
We assume here an average life expectancy of 80 years (global average: 71.5 years).

Group	Children & Young Adults	Working Age	Retired
Age Range	0-20	20-60	60-80
% of the population per age group	20 years / 80 years = 25%	40 years / 80 years = 50%	20 years / 80 years = 25%

3. POPULATION DENSITY

Density per Area

Urban	Rural
>400 people per km² (same as >1,000 per sqmile)	<400 people per km² (same as <1,000 people per sqmile)

Some key data points:

- World average: 58 inhabitants/km²
- Dhaka, Bangladesh: no.1 most dense city on the planet with 44,500 inhabitants/km²
- Mumbai, India: no.2 most dense city on the planet with 31,700 inhabitants/km²
- NYC: 10,100 inhabitants/km² with Manhattan reaching 26,000 inhabitants/km²
- Paris: 21,000 inhabitants/km²
- London: 4,500 inhabitants/km²
- Shanghai: 3,850 inhabitants/km²

Density per Country

Dense (>500 inhabitants per km²)	Low (<12 inhabitants per km²)
City-states (Monaco, Macau, Singapore, Hong-Kong, Gibraltar)	Greenland
Bangladesh	Mongolia
Taiwan	Namibia
Republic of Korea	Australia
Rwanda	Canada
The Netherlands	Russian Federation
Bangladesh	Bolivia

Source: WHO – 2015

ORDERS OF MAGNITUDE
URBAN GEOMETRY REFERENCES

1. URBAN REFERENCES

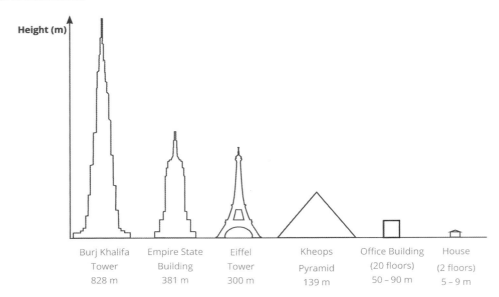

Source: Wikipedia

2. ROUGH COUNTRY/REGION SHAPES & DIMENSIONS

3. CITY SHAPES & DIMENSIONS

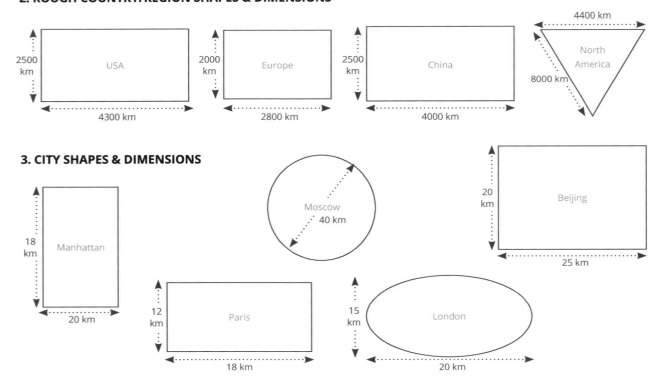

Source: Google Maps

ORDERS OF MAGNITUDE
PRODUCTIVITY REFERENCES

1. TOTAL AVAILABLE CAPACITY OR TIME

Working days

- Number of working days: 52 weeks * 5 days minus leave days = 260 days/year minus leave days
- Number of working hours per day:
  — Office work: 8 hours a day
  — In a 24/7 industry: 3 shifts of 8 hours.

Capacity limiting factors (examples)

- For a store: number of checkouts opened
- For manufacturing or industrials: number of production lines
- For consulting: number of project managers.

2. CAPACITY OR TIME REQUIRED PER EVENT (examples)

- **Fast food** – sale to serve (e.g. MacDonald's drive-thru): 1 to 3 minutes.
- **Automotive** – car assembly: 10 hours.
- **Fast fashion retailing** – design to sales floor (e.g. Zara, H&M): 10 to 15 days.
- **Shipping** – containership travel time from the UK to Hong Kong: 30 to 35 days.

ORDERS OF MAGNITUDE
CONSUMPTION REFERENCES

1. HOUSEHOLD CONSUMPTION

Average household basket of goods
(family of 4, USA, 2017)

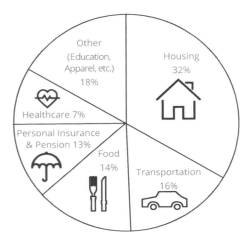

Other (Education, Apparel, etc.) 18%

Housing 32%

Healthcare 7%

Personal Insurance & Pension 13%

Food 14%

Transportation 16%

Household car usage

- Average number of cars per household: 2 (USA)
- Average fuel consumption for an individual light vehicle:
  — 56.8 miles per gallon in the EU (about 6.4L/100km)
  — 55.2 miles per gallon in the USA
  — 49.3 miles per gallon in India.

2. PRICE POINTS

Daily life

- Average USD price (**not purchase price parity**) of a Big Mac at McDonald's around the world (July 2020):
  — Switzerland: USD 6.9
  — USA (reference price): USD 5.7
  — Europe: USD 4.8
  — Brazil: USD 3.9
  — India: USD 2.5
  — South-Africa: USD 1.9

- Average public transport fare (2020)
  — NYC: USD 2.75-3
  — London: USD 3.2-6.5
  — Paris: USD 1.8-2.3
  — Shanghai: USD 0.5-1.1

Commodities (min-max, 2020)

- Oil: USD 45-65/barrel
- Gold: USD 45,000-64,500/kg
- Rice: USD 240-520/metric ton.

Sources: USA Bureau of Labor Statistics, NY Times, Forbes, The Economist – Big Mac Index – 15 July 2020, MTA, TFL, RATP, Shmetro, Business Insider, BMW, Peugeot, cse.org.uk

3. PHYSICS

Power – Electricity consumption

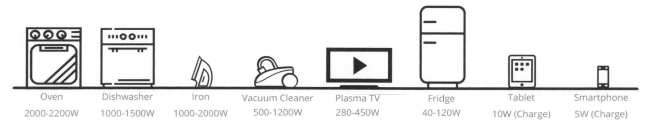

Oven	Dishwasher	Iron	Vacuum Cleaner	Plasma TV	Fridge	Tablet	Smartphone
2000-2200W	1000-1500W	1000-2000W	500-1200W	280-450W	40-120W	10W (Charge)	5W (Charge)

Approximate Densities

- Steel: 7,700 kg/m³
- Glass: 2,500 kg/m³
- Concrete: 1,500 kg/m³
- Paint: 1,300 kg/m³
- Water: 1,000 kg/m³
- Gasoline: 700 kg/m³

ECONOMIC & BUSINESS REFERENCES (1/2)

1. GDP PER CAPITA (CURRENT USD)

[USDk]

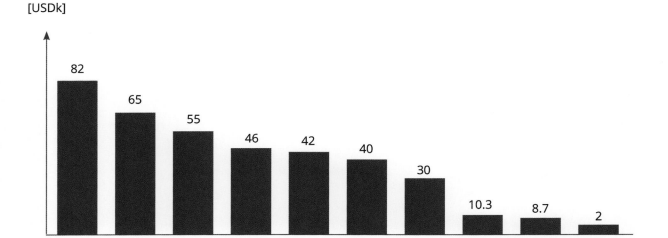

Source: World Bank Data – 2019

ORDERS OF MAGNITUDE
ECONOMIC & BUSINESS REFERENCES (2/2)

2. KEY INDUSTRIES PROFIT MARGINS & KEY COMPANIES TURNOVERS

Sector	Approximate Industry Net Profit Margin[1]	Company	Turnover (USD m)	Fiscal Year
Oil & Gas	5-10%	Sinopec Group	$407,009m	2019
		China National Petroleum Company	$379,130m	2019
		Royal Dutch Shell	$352,106m	2019
		Saudi Aramco	$329,784m	2019
		BP	$282,616m	2019
		Exxon Mobil	$264,938m	2019
Pharmaceuticals	10-30%	Johnson & Johnson	$82,059m	2019
		Roche Group	$63,434m	2019
		Bayer	$51,807m	2019
		Pfizer	$51,750m	2019
		Novartis	$50,486m	2019
Automotive	1-5%	Volkswagen Group	$282,522m	2019
		Toyota Motor	$275,288m	2019
		Daimler	$193,346m	2019
		Ford Motor	$155,900m	2019
		General Motors	$137,237m	2019
Global Beauty	1-5%	Unilever	$58,179m	2019
		L'Oreal	$33,436m	2019
		Procter & Gamble (Beauty and Grooming)	$19,096m	2019
		Colgate-Palmolive	$15,693m	2019
		The Estee Lauder Companies	$14,294m	2020
Quick Service Restaurant Companies	10-20%	McDonalds (incl. franchised restaurants)	$21,077m	2019
		Starbucks (all, incl. licensed stores)	$26,509m	2019
		Restaurant Brands International (Burger King, Tim Hortons)	$5,603m	2019
		Yum! Brands (KFC, Pizza Hut, Taco Bell)	$5,597m	2019
		Chipotle Mexican Grill	$5,586m	2019

1. Note: gross margin can be significantly higher (e.g. 60-80% in luxury).

Sector	Approximate Industry Net Profit Margin*	Company	Turnover (USD m)	Fiscal Year
Apparel Manufacturers & Retailers	1-5%	Inditex (Zara, Massimo Dutti, etc.)	$31,584m	2019
		H&M	$26,124m	2019
		Fast Retailing (Uniqlo)	$18,142m	2019
		Gap Inc. (Gap, Old Navy, Banana Republic)	$16,383m	2019
		Limited Brands (Victoria's Secrets, La Senza)	$12,914m	2019
Technology leaders	15-25%	Apple	$260,174m	2019
		Alphabet (Google)	$161,857m	2019
		Microsoft	$125,843m	2019
		Facebook	$70,697m	2019
		Netflix	$20,156m	2019
Retail	1-3%	Wal-Mart Stores	$523,964m	2019
		Amazon.com	$280,522m	2019
		Costco Wholesale Corporation	$152,703m	2019
		Target	$78,112m	2019
		Alibaba Group Holding	$73,166m	2019
		Best Buy	$43,638m	2019
Luxury Goods	10-20%	LVMH (Louis Vuitton, Bulgari, Fendi, Marc Jacobs,...)	$62,700m	2019
		Kering (Gucci, Saint Laurent, Balenciaga)	$18,600m	2019
		Compagnie Financière Richemont (Cartier, Van Cleef & Arpels, Montblanc)	$16,400m	2019
		Luxottica Group (Ray Ban, Persol, etc.)	$10,400m	2018
Airlines	1-10%[2]	Delta Air Lines	$47,007m	2019
		American Airlines Group	$45,768m	2019
		United Airlines Holdings	$43,259m	2019
		Lufthansa	$40,768m	2019
		AirFrance-KLM Group	$30,432m	2019

2. Pre-COVID
Sources: Fortune.com, Annual reports, Investors presentations, Company websites.

YOUR LOCAL ORDERS OF MAGNITUDE

1 **Fill-in this template for your country and learn these data points.**
They will help you set assumptions and conduct reality checks during your interviews.

POPULATION

- Total country population
- Average household size

Top cities	Population	Density
....	....	....
....	....	....
....	....	....

URBAN REFERENCES

- Country shape
- Country dimensions

Shape	Dimensions
....	....
....	....
....	....

PRODUCTIVITY

- Usual work day hours
- Average number of working days per year
- Average number of annual leave days

ECONOMY DATA POINTS

- GDP and GDP growth over the past two years
- Annual GDP per capita or average annual salary
- Minimal wage (if there is one)
- Corporate tax rate
- Average income tax rate
- Average inflation rate

CONSUMPTION PRICE POINTS

- Average public transport fare
- Average price for a McDonald's Big Mac
- Average price of a mobile plan (incl. data)

- Average price of 1L of milk
- Average price of 1 kg of meat (e.g. beef)
- Average price of 1kg of rice or wheat
- Average price of a cigaret pack
- Average price of a coffee
- Average price of 1 KWh
- Average price of a cinema ticket
- Average monthly price of a streaming subscription
- Average monthly price of a private health insurance
- Average price of a General Practionner appointment (GP)
- Average annual price for education in a private school

2 **List other key data points relevant for your country or your area of expertise**

Where to find the data?

You should be able to find everything online. Check for instance:

- data.worldbank.org
- www.data.ocde.org
- www.cia.gov
- Local Ministry of Economy website (inflation, GDO/GDP, budget)
- Local statistics body (household and consumption datapoints)
- Your utility/phone invoices
- Your tax/payroll statements
- Private providers websites.

OTHER KEY DIMENSIONS

CHAPTER 9
QUANT SKILLS
TIPS TO HELP YOU TACKLE QUANTITATIVE BUSINESS PROBLEMS UNDER PRESSURE

During the case study, **the interviewer will usually test your calculation skills**.

Performing calculations in front of someone is totally different from calculating on your own, with plenty of time. For many candidates, it becomes the most stressful moment of the interview.

To cope with the pressure, you need to be confident you know how to tackle the question.

This chapter will help you by summarizing all the **basic and more advanced math concepts you should be familiar with.**

However, this is not enough. You also need to **be familiar identifying which math concept applies** when hearing a quantitative business problem.

You will thus find in this chapter **practice exercises to apply math concepts in a business context.**

PRACTICE

+

BREATHING

=

SUCCESS

REQUIRED
🦉 BASIC ARITHMETIC

INTERVIEWERS WILL TEST YOUR ABILITY TO DO BASIC CALCULATIONS. REVIEW THE CALCULATION TIPS BELOW AND PRACTICE WITH THE SHORT DRY RUN QUESTIONS.

See answers page 252.

ADDITIONS

- Round numbers to multiples of 10 or 5 and subtract what you added.

$$308 + 128 = 310 + 130 - 2 - 2 = 440 - 4 = 436$$

DRY RUN 1: Company X has USD 105m fixed costs and USD 198m variable costs per year; what is the total cost base?

SUBTRACTIONS

- Some candidates struggle with subtractions where the difference is negative. In these cases, take the opposite and add a negative sign.

$$120 - 209? \rightarrow 209 - 120 = 89 \rightarrow -89$$

**DRY RUN 2: Company Y generated EUR 950m in revenue and had a EUR 1.92bn operating cost-base.
What is their operating loss in EUR bn?**

MULTIPLICATIONS AND CROSS-MULTIPLICATIONS

- Practice multiplications on paper
- To multiply by 15, multiply first by 10, then divide by 2 and add everything.

$$15 \times 120 = 1200 + \frac{1200}{2} = 1800$$

- To multiply by 25, multiply by 100 then divide by 4.
- If you don't write multiplications on paper, you can break them down as the sum or difference of simpler multiplications.

$$18 * 21 = (20 - 2) * (20 + 1)$$

DRY RUN 3: Company W has a 29% market share in a 38bn market. How much revenue do they make?

- If $A \rightarrow \text{Value}_1$ and $B \rightarrow \text{Value}_2$ then $B = \frac{Value_2}{Value_1} * A$.

$$\text{Revenue}_1 \rightarrow \text{Profit}_1 \text{ and } \text{Revenue}_2 \rightarrow \text{Profit}_2$$
$$\Rightarrow \text{Profit}_2 = \text{Profit}_1 * \frac{\text{Revenue}_2}{\text{Revenue}_1}$$

DRY RUN 4: Company W generated 800m profit out of a 2bn revenue. What would be its profit if the profit margin was unchanged but revenue down to 1.5bn?

DIVISIONS AND PERCENTAGES

- Practice divisions on paper.
- To divide by 5, multiply by 2 and divide by 10.
- Whenever possible, turn the division into a simple fraction and use the shortcuts below.

$$5/7 \times 120 = 5 \times 1/7 \times 120 = 5 \times 0.14 \times 120 = 0.7 \times 120$$

FRACTION	APPROXIMATE VALUE
1/2	0.50
1/3	0.33
1/4	0.25
1/5	0.20
1/6	0.17
1/7	0.14
1/8	0.13
1/9	0.11

DRY RUN 5: Company Z's revenue was GBP 800m and their cost base GBP 500m.
What percentage of the revenue does the cost base represent?

WEIGHTED AVERAGES

- For an average to be weighted, you need to multiply each percentage by its weight, add these and then divide by the sum of weights.
  - Note: when you hear that % A is n-th times % B, the sum of weights (the divisor) is equal to (n+1) — see example below.

DRY RUN 6: Company Y has a 20% market share in the US and 15% market share in Canada and Mexico. The US market is twice as big as the Canadian and Mexican markets combined.
What is Company Y market share across Northern-America?

GCD AND LCM (MORE ADVANCED)

- Use a greatest common divisor – GCD – to find the maximum number of bundles with 2 or more items.

DRY RUN 7: What is the maximum number of gift boxes one can prepare with 2,000 dark chocolate balls and 3,500 milk ones?

- Use a least common multiple – LCM – to find the minimum amount required for 2 or more things to sync or align.

DRY RUN 8: Two production lines – A and B – start simultaneously. Line A takes 8 minutes to run, whereas line B needs 28 minutes.
When will both finish their production cycle at the same time?

REQUIRED
ZEROS AND POWERS

IT IS VERY EASY TO MAKE A CALCULATION MISTAKE BY FORGETTING OR ADDING AN EXTRA ZERO WHEN MULTIPLYING NUMBERS, E.G. TO SIZE A MARKET OR WHEN DEALING WITH UNITS.

REVIEW THE CALCULATION TIPS BELOW AND PRACTICE WITH THE SHORT DRY RUN QUESTIONS.

See answers page 253.

POWERS OF 10

- **Don't "write all the zeros".** It is slow and you will make a mistake.
- **Use powers of 10 as much as possible.**

$$1,200 \times \frac{10,000}{60,000} = \frac{12 \times 10^2 \times 10^4}{6 \times 10^4} = 2 \times 10^2 = 200$$

- Add the powers when you multiply.

$$10^3 \times 10^5 = 10^8$$

- Subtract them when you divide.

$$\frac{10^3}{10^5} = 10^{-2} = 0.01$$

- It is common to state a frequency in the population as a number of cases per 100,000 inhabitants. To have the total number of cases, multiply by the population and again by 10^{-5}.

   DRY RUN 9: Country X has 20 million inhabitants and its death rate is 15 per 100,000. How many people passed away this year?

   DRY RUN 10: A company is valued by DCF and its terminal value parameters are a USD 5m annual FCF in the previous year, a 2% perpetual growth rate and a 3% company WACC. What is the terminal value?

SQUARES

- Know the first 20 squares.

n	n^2	n	n^2	n	n^2	n	n^2
1	1	6	36	11	121	16	256
2	4	7	49	12	144	17	289
3	9	8	64	13	169	18	324
4	16	9	81	14	196	19	361
5	25	10	100	15	225	20	400

UNITS

- Interviewers sometimes set up traps by having you deal with multiple units. In this case, consider using the international standards units:
  - — Weight: gram
  - — Length: meter
  - — Time: second.

- Note: for energy calculations, it is often easier to use Watts for power and Watt-hours Wh for Energy (Power in Watts * number of hours = Energy in Watt-hours).

> **DRY RUN 11: How much electricity in kWh does a company consume per year with a 1000W appliance used half of the day every day?**

> **DRY RUN 12: What is the rough number of campervans that could fit in a 20 acres camping, if the average campervan requires about 100 sqm?**

> **DRY RUN 13: What is the oil equivalent (in terms of energy i.e. in BOEs) of the 4,800,000 cubic feet of natural gas contained in a liquefied natural gas vessel?**

SQUARE ROOTS

- Be comfortable manipulating square roots, if needed — e.g. for a CAGR or a Discounted Cash Flow.

$\sqrt{n}$	(APPROXIMATE) VALUE
$\sqrt{A \times B}$	$\sqrt{A} \times \sqrt{B}$
$\sqrt{\frac{A}{B}}$	$\frac{\sqrt{A}}{\sqrt{B}}$
$\sqrt{100}$	10
$\sqrt{25}$	5
$\sqrt{10}$	3.16
$\sqrt{9}$	3
$\sqrt{5}$	2.23
$\sqrt{3}$	1.73
$\sqrt{2}$	1.41
$\sqrt{1}$	1

> **DRY RUN 14: If a company grows from USD 5m in year 0 to 10m in year 4, what is the CAGR over that period?**

REQUIRED

GEOMETRY

SOME SIZING PROBLEMS CAN BE EASILY SOLVED THANKS TO GEOMETRIC APPROXIMATIONS.
YOU THUS NEED TO KNOW SOME BASIC AND MORE ADVANCED FORMULAS.

SQUARE WITH SIDE c

Perimeter: sum of all sides $= 4 \times c$

Area: c^2

RECTANGLE WITH SIDES L AND l

Perimeter: sum of all sides $= 2 \times (L + l)$

Area: $L \times l$

TRIANGLE WITH BASE b AND HEIGHT h

Perimeter: sum of all sides

Area: $\frac{b \times h}{2}$

DISC/CIRCLE WITH A RADIUS r

Circumference: $2 \times \pi \times r$

Area: $\pi \times r^2$

$\pi \approx 3.14$

RHOMBUS WITH DIAGONALS $d1$ AND $d2$, AND SIDE a

Perimeter: $4 \times a$

Area: $\frac{d1 \times d2}{2}$

ELLIPSE WITH SEMI-MINOR AXIS a AND SEMI-MAJOR AXIS b

Area: $\pi \times a \times b$

Note: the ellipse circumference cannot be calculated simply.

RIGHT-ANGLED TRIANGLE WITH SMALLER SIDES a, b AND HYPOTENUSE c

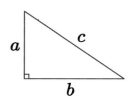

$$c = \sqrt{a^2 + b^2}$$

SPHERE/BALL WITH A RADIUS r

External area: $4 \times \pi \times r^2$

Volume: $4/3 \times \pi \times r^3$

TUBE/EMPTY CYLINDER WITH RADIUS r AND HEIGHT h

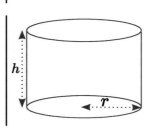

External area: $2 \times \pi \times r \times h$

Volume: $\pi \times r^2 \times h$

CUBE WITH SIDES c

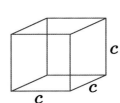

External area: $6 \times c^2$

Volume: c^3

TRIANGULAR PRISM WITH TRIANGLE SIDES a,b,c, HEIGHT h AND ALTITUDE H

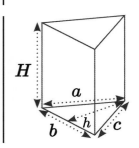

External area: $H \times (a + b + c) + b \times h$

Volume: $H \times b \times h / 2$

CONE WITH RADIUS r, HEIGHT h AND SLANT HEIGHT L

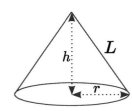

External area: $\pi \times r^2 + \pi \times r \times L$

Volume: $1/3 \times \pi \times r^2 \times h$

NICE TO KNOW
ANALYSIS AND CALCULUS (1/2)

WE WILL INTRODUCE IN THE FOLLOWING PAGES SOME MORE ADVANCED MATHEMATICAL TOOLS WHICH CAN HELP YOU IN QUANTITATIVE PROBLEMS.

THEY CAN NOTABLY HELP YOU DESCRIBE REAL-LIFE PHENOMENA.

See answers page 254.

LOGARITHM

- Some charts aim to show data points with very different numbers. In this case, it is sometimes helpful to use a logarithmic scale.
- The logarithm function $\log(x)$ basically gives the power of the power of 10, e.g. if the value we want to plot is $x = 1,000,000 = 10^6$, then $\log(x) = 6$.
- Each unit step on the scale is called a "decade". Note it is subdivided in smaller steps which are distributed in a non-linear way.

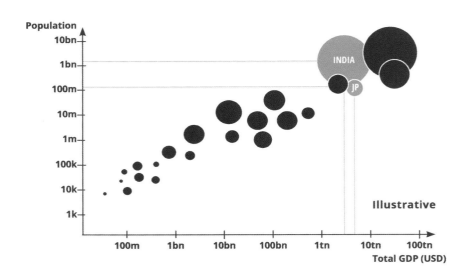

DRY RUN 15: Based on the chart above, how much higher is approximately the Japanese GDP/capita compared to the Indian one?

PRIMITIVE AND DERIVATIVE (SPEED)

- In physics, speed is the derivative of a movement. The same applies to business metrics, e.g.:
  - If sales grow at a steady rate, the sales growth rate is a constant k and the function describing sales is the primitive, i.e. $f(month) = k \times month + C$ where C is the sales in month 0.
  - Similarly, if the sales growth rate doubles every year, the function describing sales is its primitive i.e. $x^2 + C$.

DRY RUN 16: Company X generated EUR 15m in 2015. It grew by +2% in 2016 and maintained this revenue increase in dollars in following years. How much revenue did the company generate in 2018?

INTEGRAL (SUM)

- To calculate the cumulative amount over time for a value described by a continuous function (e.g. cumulative sales), calculate its integral (area under the curve).

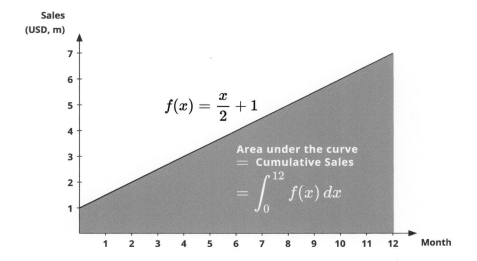

DRY RUN 17: In the example above (chart), how much revenue was generated in the second half of the year (H2)?

NICE TO KNOW
ANALYSIS AND CALCULUS (2/2)

See answers page 254.

EXPONENTIAL DECAY

- Exponential decay functions are also helpful to model some life or business phenomena.

$$f(t) = C \times (1 - e^{-t/\tau})$$

$$f(t) = k * e^{-t/\tau}$$

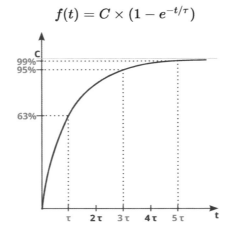

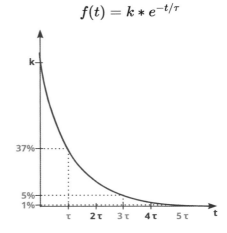

- The "growing and slowing" function is $f(t) = C - k \times e^{-t/\tau}$ where C is the cap, k a factor defining the value for t=0, and τ the time constant (i.e. the mean lifetime).
- If the function is equal to 0 for t=0 (see chart above), then $k = C$ and $f(t) = C \times (1 - e^{-t/\tau})$.
- In this case:

  $f(\tau)$ equals approx. 63% of $C = k$

  $f(3\tau)$ equals approx. 95% of $C = k$

  $f(5\tau)$ equals approx. 99% of $C = k$

- The "decreasing and slowing" function from a value k at t=0 is $f(t) = k * e^{-t/\tau}$.
- In this case:

  $f(\tau)$ equals approx. 37% of k

  $f(3\tau)$ equals approx. 5% of k

  $f(5\tau)$ equals approx. 1% of k

- In both cases, the time needed to reach 50% of the maximum value is called the half-life:

$$t_{1/2} = \tau \times ln(2) \approx 0.7 \times \tau \qquad \tau = \frac{t_{1/2}}{ln(2)} \approx 1.44 \times t_{1/2}$$

DRY RUN 18: Company Z starts clearance sales on cooking robots on Saturday. Thanks to effective promotion, most units are sold in the first few days, following an exponential decay curve. After 5 days half of units are sold. How long will it take to sell all units?

ALGEBRA (1/2)

See answers page 255.

ARITHMETIC PROGRESSIONS

- Arithmetic progressions are series of numbers with a common difference d. The n-th term u_n equals:

$$u_n = u_0 + n \times d$$

- The sum of the first n terms of the arithmetic progression equals:

$$\sum_{k=0}^{n} u_k = \frac{(n+1) \times (\text{first term} + \text{n-th term})}{2} = \frac{(n+1) \times (2 \times u_0 + n \times d)}{2}$$

- When the progression is the sum of integers 1, 2, 3..., it becomes:

$$\sum_{k=1}^{n} k = \frac{(n+1) \times (n+2)}{2}$$

DRY RUN 19: A social network startup starts with 50 people and acquires 100 more people every month.
How many people are part of the network after 6 months?

GEOMETRIC PROGRESSIONS

- Geometric progressions are series of numbers with a common scale factor q. The n-th term u_n equals:

$$u_n = u_0 \times q^n$$

— E.g. the company revenue grows 5% year-on-year:

$$revenue_{\text{year\_n}} = revenue_{\text{year\_0}} \times (1.05)^n$$

- The sum of the first n terms of the geometric progression equals:

$$\sum_{k=0}^{n} u_k = u_0 \times \frac{1 - q^{n+1}}{1 - q}; \text{ with } q \neq 1$$

DRY RUN 20: Company Z has constant Free Cash Flows (FCF). What is the DCF formula until year n?

NICE TO KNOW
ALGEBRA (2/2)

See answers page 255.

LINEAR EQUATIONS

- You should also be comfortable solving linear equations or systems of linear equations, e.g.:
  — We can easily find a volume breakeven point, knowing that:

$$\text{revenue} = \text{unit price} \times \text{units sold} \qquad \text{(a)}$$
$$\text{costs} = \text{fixed costs} + \text{unit cost} \times \text{units sold} \qquad \text{(b)}$$

  — By writing the equation below:

$$\text{Profit} = 0 = \text{revenue} - \text{costs} \qquad \text{(a-b)}$$
$$= (\text{unit price} - \text{unit costs}) \times \text{units sold} - \text{fixed costs}$$
$$\rightarrow \text{units sold} = \frac{\text{fixed costs}}{\text{unit price} - \text{unit costs}}$$

DRY RUN 21: Find the number of movies above which it becomes more interesting to pay an annual USD 200 membership fee to access any movies, rather than simply pay a USD 15 ticket without membership.

STATISTICS AND PROBABILITY (1/2)

See answers page 256.

PROBABILITIES

- A few basic probability rules must be known.
  If two events A and B are independent and have a respective probability of occurrence P(A) and P(B) then:
  — The probability of the two events happening is:

  P(A and B) = P(A) * P(B)

  — The probability of at least one of the events happening is:

  P(A or B) = P(A) + P(B) – P(A and B)

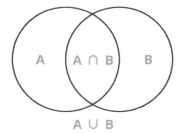

DRY RUN 22: 40% have hypertension, 20% have diabetes. 10% have both. What is the probability of having either hypertension or diabetes?

**STATISTICAL
DISTRIBUTIONS**

- In statistics, events can be modeled following many types of distribution but practically, in consulting, we only use a few distributions:
  — **UNIFORM**: the variable can take any value between a min and a max with the same probability
  — **NORMAL (BELL CURVE).** E.g. time to complete a task, performance

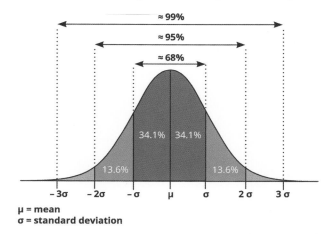

μ = mean
σ = standard deviation

If μ is the average (mean) value and σ is the standard deviation:

- **Approx. 68% of the population is between [μ – σ; μ + σ]**
- **Approx. 95% of the population is between [μ – 2 σ; μ + 2 σ]**
- **Approx. 99% of the population is between [μ – 3 σ; μ + 3 σ]**

  — **BINOMIAL,** when we test the probability for independent tests having **2 potential values** (e.g. success or failure like in a quality sampling).

Probability P of k successes after n tests, with p the probability of success for one test:

$$P = \binom{n}{k} \times p^k \times (1-p)^{n-k}; \text{ with the binomial coefficient } \frac{n!}{k! \times (n-k)!}$$

Note: a very large number of tests leads to a normal distribution.

DRY RUN 23: An airline company noticed that 10% of its customers do not show up for their flight. It decides to accept up to 98 bookings for 95 seats. If 98 bookings were made on a flight, what is the formula giving the probability that everyone showing up gets a seat?

NICE TO KNOW
STATISTICS AND PROBABILITY (2/2)

See answers page 256.

COMBINATORICS

- Combinatorics can be helpful to quantify the number of possibilities for business options (e.g. number of products with different colors for different components).
- A number of formulas involve the **factorial** ($n!$), which is equal to the **product of integers** from 1 to n.

> **E.g.** $5! = 1 \times 2 \times 3 \times 4 \times 5 = 120$

- Key cases and formulas include:
  — **Permutations** of k elements taken in n elements, **without repetition.**

  > **E.g. ranking top 3 employees**
  > $$\frac{n!}{(n-k)!}$$

  — **Permutations** of k elements taken in n elements, **with repetitions.**

  > **E.g. phone PIN code (order matters but you can repeat numbers)**
  > $$n^k$$

  — If the **order does not matter**, the number of **combinations without repetition** equals the **binomial coefficient.**

  > **E.g. lottery draw**
  > $$\binom{n}{k} = \frac{n!}{k! \times (n-k)!}$$

  — Lastly, if the **order does not matter and we can repeat** values:

  > **E.g. number of possible ways to order multiple drinks at the bar (if you receive two beers then three gin and tonic, it is the same as three gin and tonic and two beers)**
  > $$\frac{(n+k-1)!}{k! \times (n-1)!}$$

> **DRY RUN 24: A TelCo company sells bundles of 3 products out of its 5 products. How many bundles are there?**

STRATINTERVIEWS

PRACTICE CALCULATIONS UNDER TIME PRESSURE TO
INCREASE YOUR CONFIDENCE

_____

HOW DOES IT WORK?

1

LISTEN TO THE INTERVIEWER

You will go through a first series of purely mathematical questions, to ensure you master the key concepts.

You will then practice translating quantitative business problems into mathematical concepts, to be sharp in the interviews.

2

CALCULATE & SUBMIT YOUR ANSWER

Your time to answer is limited, replicating the pressure experienced in strategy interviews.

Breathe, caculate leveraging the tips we just reviewed, then submit your answer.

3

CHECK YOUR STRENGTHS & WEAKNESSES

After completing a series, you will have access to a summary page with answers, as well as your score for each quantitative skill or concept.

This allows you to focus your preparation efforts ahead of the next series.

Practice on
www.stratinterviews.com

CHAPTER 10
FIT AND MOTIVATION
WHAT TO ASK, WHAT TO SAY AND HOW TO BEHAVE WHEN INTERVIEWED

While a significant part of the interview aims to assess whether you have the hard skills to be a consultant, **interviewers also decide whether they would like you to be joining the office** and working with them on a daily basis.

In a nutshell, firms expect you to **be constantly professional and genuinely nice**.

It is not unusual to cover fit questions at the back, after the case study, as it is at that moment that the candidates relax and tend to reveal their true selves.

Don't get caught off-guard:

- Do your homework beforehand to **answer basic and tricky questions**.
- **Practice your storytelling** to make sure it is as compelling as an executive summary: crisp, robust, impactful.
- **Stay focused** and engaged in the conversation.
- **Be professional** with everyone, before and after the interviews.

This chapter will give you an idea of some of the **traps to avoid** and will give you some guidance on what to prepare and do or not do.

DO NOT IMPROVISE

&

STAY

FOCUSED

QUESTIONS ABOUT YOU

EVEN THOUGH THE INTERVIEW MAY BE MORE RELAXED AFTER THE CASE, THE FIT AND MOTIVATION QUESTIONS SECTION CAN DRIVE A YES OR A "DING":

- Keep the same energy level and structure when answering.
- Show what a nice person you are.

WHY FIT QUESTIONS?

Fit questions have various purposes:

- Filter out candidates that do not have a clear understanding of consulting and a clear rationale for joining strategy firms.
- Understand how you make decisions.
- Understand what drives you.
- Test your resilience and ability to remain structured in every circumstance.
- Last but not least, try to get to know the *real you*, beneath the perfect candidate you will have tried to be during the interview.

For each fit question, prepare and write down your structure, then practice telling the story in a natural way:

- Stick to 2 or 3 MECE arguments.
- Support them with one or two concrete examples if possible.
- Aim for 2 minutes maximum per answer.

1 MINIMUM HOMEWORK

Be ready to answer questions about:

- **Why consulting?**
  - Why does it make sense considering your previous experience and your vision for your career?

- **Why join this firm** (and not our competitors)?
  - Interviewers can ask you where else you applied and you must be ready to explain why.

- **Will you be succesful** in this firm?
  - Be clear on the skills required to succeed as a junior/senior consultant and demonstrate concisely that you master these.

- **Why choose you** (and not another candidate)?
  - Pick the most differentiating points, e.g. your unique experience, skills, etc.

Prepare as well **situational questions**, e.g.

- When did you achieve more than expected?
- Tell us about a time when you did not meet expectations
- Tell us about a time when you had a conflict.
- Tell us about a time when you had to confront someone for something important.
- How do you obtain something from someone you don't manage directly?
- How would you deal with a client telling you your work is wrong and threatening to call the Partner to cancel the project?

2 QUESTIONS YOU WANT TO AVOID

Consultants too prepare the interview. They notably read your resume (and cover letter at times) and think about the 2 or 3 questions that will be difficult for you to answer.

List the **2 or 3 questions that would make you uncomfortable and absolutely prepare an answer**. This will significantly increase your level of confidence.

RANDOM/PROVOCATIVE QUESTIONS

Consultants can ask you random, purposefully provocative or even inappropriate questions, to **test your resilience and poise.**

Breathe. Don't take these personnally. Do not become an activist if the topic matters to you. **Try to respond like a consultant**, i.e. articulating the options, assessing pros & cons and getting to a logical, balanced answer.

PRACTICE & IMPROVE

FILL-IN THE TEMPLATE BELOW FOR EACH OF THE QUESTIONS IDENTIFIED ON THE PREVIOUS PAGE. THEN, PRACTICE TELLING THAT STORY IN A CONCISE, COMPELLING WAY.

 TEMPLATE

FIT/MOTIVATION QUESTIONS PREP

QUESTION • …

KEY MESSAGES/ARGUMENTS	ILLUSTRATION/EXAMPLE
1. • …	1. • …
2. • …	2. • …
3. • …	3. • …

STRATINTERVIEWS

PRACTICE CALCULATIONS UNDER TIME PRESSURE TO
INCREASE YOUR CONFIDENCE

HOW DOES IT WORK?

1

RECORD YOUR ANSWERS

Listen to the interviewer's question and record your answer.

You will go through a series of questions, covering both the basics and the more challenging questions we were asked or that we asked as interviewers.

2

FINE-TUNE YOUR ANSWERS TO EACH QUESTION

Review your videos to see if the flow is natural, concise and compelling.

Read our solving tips then jot down the key points and examples you want to convey.

3

PRACTICE TELLING YOUR STORY

You can record yourself again as many times as you want and need, until you make it perfect.

Focus on your body language, and take the opportunity to optimize your set-up if you are interviewing from home.

Practice on
www.stratinterviews.com

QUESTIONS TO INTERVIEWERS

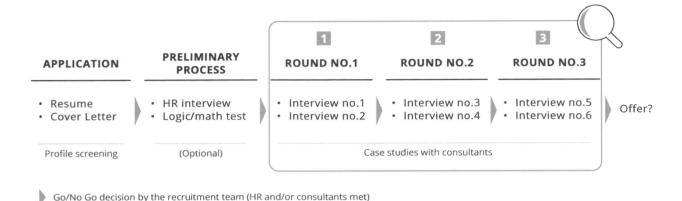

APPLICATION	PRELIMINARY PROCESS	**1** ROUND NO.1	**2** ROUND NO.2	**3** ROUND NO.3	
• Resume • Cover Letter	• HR interview • Logic/math test	• Interview no.1 • Interview no.2	• Interview no.3 • Interview no.4	• Interview no.5 • Interview no.6	Offer?
Profile screening	(Optional)		Case studies with consultants		

▶ Go/No Go decision by the recruitment team (HR and/or consultants met)

You will have the opportunity to ask a few questions at the back of the interview — aim to ask at least 2 and potentially more if you have time or feel the interviewer is keen to continue.

The input you receive should help you strengthen your story in the next round.

List the 5-6 questions you would like to ask in each round. Note that it is not unusual for consultants to capture the questions you asked, so change questions from one round to another.

The interviewers will usually start the meeting by introducing themselves. Listen and take notes about their profile to be able to leverage this for your questions at the back of the interview.

Be genuinely interested in what the interviewers say (don't ask a question without listening to the answer because you are preparing your next question).

1 ROUND 1

Get Junior/Senior Consultants to talk about their experience – building on their intro – and give you insights on the firm's business, e.g.:

- How did you get to join this firm?
- Which types of projects did you work on? What is the project you preferred and what is the worst one?
- What excites you most in your work?
- What are the most important industries in terms of revenue or number of partners?
- What does your typical week look like?
- What do you find is the most difficult in your work?

Leverage your company profile (see page 48) to ideate questions.
Keep a record as well of your interviews and of the questions asked on both sides (see below).

TEMPLATE – INTERVIEW TRACKING

FIRM – OFFICE	○
INTERVIEW DATE	INTERVIEW TRACKING

	INTERVIEWER's QUESTIONS	MY QUESTIONS
INTERVIEWER's NAME		
SENIORITY	• ... • ... • ...	• ... • ... • ...
EMAIL		

2 ROUND 2

Elevate the conversation with Managers to prepare for Partners interviews, e.g.:

- What do you expect from a junior consultant? What makes the difference between the good consultant and the very good consultant?
- What do you find unique to this firm?
- What makes you stay?
- How do you see the firm evolve over the next few years?
- What are the key challenges and opportunities for the firm?
- When were you proud/did you have the feeling you made an impact?

3 ROUND 3

Convey to Partners that you have the maturity and drive required to be successful in the long run, e.g.:

- What is the growth ambition for the firm?
- What are the key challenges and opportunities for the firm?
- Have you identified specific capabilities that will be required to achieve this ambition?
- What would be your advice for me if I joined the firm?

Note: asking for direct feedback face-to-face at the end of the interview is risky because you put the interviewer on the spot while they might still be hesitating.
Giving you feedback live will influence the decision.

A FEW EXTRA PRACTICAL TIPS

BE NICE WITH EVERYONE

HR or assistants who invite you via phone or email **will let interviewers know** if you were nice or rude, made mistakes – including typos – or if you made their lives difficult during the scheduling process. Hence:

- Be courteous and accommodating.
- Try to avoid postponing interviews with Partners. Finding time-slots working with them is difficult and it puts you at risk of being deprioritized.

LOOK PROFESSIONAL

Interviewers expect you to come to the interview with a **professional look** as if you were joining a client meeting. Too often, interviewers are negatively distracted. Here are a few suggestions:

- Men should wear a tie.
- Avoid creative, fashionable, gaudy colors. Stick to classic white/blue.
- Don't come overdressed and don't attempt to be original, e.g. bow tie, handkerchief, jewelry...
- Avoid excessive make-up and perfume (or sweat...).

Wear a **watch** to see how you are doing with time (turn off email alerts if it is a smartwatch).

WHAT TO BRING?

Bring **2 copies of your resume**, in case the interviewers misplaced their copies. The fact that your printer has an ink cartridge issue is not a valid reason for bringing a resume printed in yellow — it unfortunately happens...

Bring your own A4 white sheets, pencil and calculator. A4 sheets allow you to sketch a diagram or powerpoint slide and hand it over, without showing your notes.

You might be allowed to use a calculator. The interviewer might provide you with one – some firms do that – but be prepared to do pen and paper calculations.

If you are invited for a case study preparation or computer-based test, don't hesitate to bring earplugs — recruitment areas can be noisy.

BE PUNCTUAL

You should be at reception **10-15 min. in advance** to allow for a potential visitor sign-in process.

To **avoid any unnecessary stress, plan your trip in advance**. Check travel time and alternative travel options (in case your bus or train gets stuck in traffic). Check on Google StreetView what the building looks like. This will help you **visualize and mentally prepare** for the interview.

AT THE START OF THE INTERVIEW

Put your **phone on plane mode**. Note that **interviewers might check their phone** during the interview. It is not meant to be rude and it does not mean you are performing badly. There are just client emergencies sometimes.

If you can, choose a **seat** considering:

- Sunlight: interviewers want to see your face but you do not want to bake.
- Where the interviewer sits: if the table is round, avoid being directly in front of the interviewer and sit slightly closer to be able to engage more (e.g. explaining your approach, your equation or your recommendation).

If you are offered a drink, either politely decline or accept something simple, that doesn't waste time (a glass of water is usually a good call).

AFTER THE INTERVIEW

You can send a concise thank-you email after the interview, but it will likely not influence the interviewer's judgment.

The **best candidates send a thank you email when they already know they go to the next round and take this opportunity to ask for feedback** and tips for the next rounds. This is smart because if the consultants sent you to the next round it means they support you and will try to help by telling you (part of) what they have told your next interviewers.

If you have the opportunity to meet or speak with HR/an assistant again, **continue to be nice** to them. HR can have their say (positive or negative) for the final offer decision and assistants will have an influence on the timing of your next interviews.

Note: often Partner interviews will include a discussion on your **performance in earlier stages**. Be prepared to list things that went well and things that were less easy. Be factual and accurate but don't over-emphasize problems as you do not want to make Partners hesitate.

APPENDIX

QUANT SOLUTIONS – REQUIRED QUANT
BASIC ARITHMETIC

1. Company X has USD 105m fixed costs and USD 198m variable costs per year. What is the total cost base?

$$105 + 198 = 105 + 200 - 2 = 305 - 2 = \text{USD } 303m$$

2. Company Y generated EUR 950m in revenue and had a EUR 1.92bn operating cost-base. What is their operating loss in EUR bn?

$$950m - 1.92bn = -(1.92 - 0.95) = -(0.97) \rightarrow \text{EUR } 0.97bn \text{ loss}$$

3. Company W has a 29% market share in a 38bn market. How much revenue do they make?

$$29 \times 38 = (30 - 1) \times (40 - 2) = 30 \times 40 - 40 - 30 \times 2 + 2 = 1200 - 100 + 2 = 1102 \rightarrow 11.02bn$$

4. Company W generated 800m profit out of a 2bn revenue. What would be its profit if the profit margin was unchanged but revenue down to 1.5bn?

$$800 * \frac{1.5}{2} = 600m$$

5. Company Z's revenue was GBP 800m and their cost base GBP 500m. What percentage of the revenue does the cost base represent?

$$500/800 = 5 * 1/8 \approx 5 * 0.13 \approx 0.65 \rightarrow \sim 65\%$$

6. Company Y has a 20% market share in the US and 15% market share in Canada and Mexico. The US market is twice as big as the Canadian and Mexican markets combined. What is Company Y market share across Northern-America?

$$[20\% * 2 \text{ (US)} + 15\% * 1 \text{ (CA+MEX)}]/[2 + 1] = [40\% + 15\%]/3 = 55\%/3 \approx 18.3\% \text{ on average}$$

7. What is the maximum number of gift boxes one can prepare with 2,000 dark chocolate balls and 3,500 milk ones, minimizing wastage?

GCD(2,000; 3,500) = 500.

Each gift box will contain 4 (2,000 / 500) dark and 7 (3,500 / 500) milk chocolate balls.

8. Two production lines – A and B – start simultaneously. Line A takes 8 minutes to run, whereas line B needs 28 minutes. When will both finish their production cycle at the same time?

LCM(8; 28) = LCM(2^3; $2^2 \times 7$) = $2^3 \times 7$ = 56. Every 56 minutes

ZEROS AND POWERS

**9. Country X has 20 million inhabitants and its death rate is 15 per 100,000.
How many people passed away this year?**

$$15 * 10^{-5} * 2 * 10^7 = 30 * 10^2 = 3000$$

**10. A company is valued by DCF and its terminal value parameters are a USD 5m annual FCF in the previous year, a 2% perpetual growth rate and a 3% company WACC.
What is the terminal value?**

$$TV = 5m * (1 + 2\%)/(3\% - 2\%) = 5.1 * 10^6 * 10^2 = \text{USD } 510m$$

Refer to Company Valuation Methods page 124 for more details on the method

11. How much electricity in kWh does a company consume per year with a 1000W appliance used half of the day every day?

$$1\text{kW} * 12\text{h} * 365 \text{ days} = 3650 + 730 = 4380\text{kWh}$$

12. What is the rough number of campervans that could fit in a 20 acres camping if the average campervan requires about 100 sqm?

$$\approx 20 * 4047/100 \approx 810 \text{ campervans}$$

13. What is the oil equivalent (in terms of energy) of the 4,800,000 cubic feet of natural gas contained in a liquefied natural gas vessel?

One Barrel of Oil Equivalent (BOE) is equivalent to approx. 6000 cubic feet of natural gas so the vessel contains:

$$48 * \frac{10^5}{6*10^3} = 8 * 10^2 = 800 \text{ BOE}$$

(note : a BOE is equivalent to 1,700 kWh)

14. If a company grows from USD 5m in year 0 to 10m in year 4, what is the CAGR over that period?

$$CAGR = (\frac{10}{5})^{\frac{1}{4}} - 1 = \sqrt{\sqrt{2}} - 1 \approx \sqrt{1.4} - 1$$

$\sqrt{1.4}$ is between 1 ($\sqrt{1}$) and 1.4 so roughly 1.2 i.e. 20% CAGR (actual value is approximately 19%).

QUANT SOLUTIONS – NICE TO KNOW QUANT
ANALYSIS AND CALCULUS

15. Based on the chart page 232, how much higher is approximately the Japanese GDP/capita compared to the Indian one?

The Japanese GDP is approximately twice the Indian GDP (≈ 5 Tn vs. 2.5 Tn), i.e. a 2-to-1 ratio.
The Japanese population is approximately a tenth of the Indian one, i.e. a 1-to-10 ratio.

$$\frac{2/1}{1/10} = 20 \text{ times higher approximately}$$

16. Company X generated EUR 15m in 2015. It grew by +2% in 2016 and maintained this revenue increase in dollars in following years. How much revenue did the company generate in 2018?

The growth rate function is: $f'(year) = 0.02 \times 15$ (constant function).Its primitive is:
$f(year) = 0.02 \times 15 \times year + C$ (Constant).

We know that: $f(2015) = 15m = 0.02 \times 15 \times 2015 + C \;\rightarrow C = 15 \times (1 - 0.02 \times 2015)$

$\rightarrow f(year) = 15 + 0.02 \times 15 \times (year - 2015)$

$\rightarrow f(2018) = 15 + 0.02 \times 15 \times 3$

Note: this is a trivial example to illustrate primitives; in an interview, we would expect you to directly say that
$f(2018) = 15 + 0.02 \times 15 \times 3$

17. In the chart page 233, how much revenue was generated in the second half of the year?

Sales are modeled (in USD m) by the function $f(x) = \frac{x}{2} + 1$. Cumulative sales in H2 equal:

$$\int_{x=6}^{12} (\tfrac{x}{2} + 1)dx = \left[\tfrac{x^2}{4} + x \right]_6^{12} = \tfrac{144-36}{4} + 12 - 6 = \tfrac{108}{4} + 6 = \text{ USD } 33m$$

Note: in this simple linear example you could have reached the same result with a geometric approach, adding up a 6 x 4 = 24m rectangle to a right-angle triangle (6 x 3/2 = 9m).

18. Company Z starts clearance sales on cooking robots on Saturday. Thanks to effective promotion, most units are sold in the first few days, following an exponential decay curve. After 5 days half of units are sold. How long will it take to sell all units?

Mathematically speaking, units will never all be sold as the exponential function will never reach 0. However we can approximate with 99% of units which we know occurs after:

$$5 \times \tau = \frac{t_{1/2}}{ln(2)} \approx 5 \times 1.44 \times 5 \text{ days } \approx 36 \text{ days}$$

ALGEBRA

19. A social network startup starts with 50 people and acquires 100 more people every month. How many people are part of the network after 6 months?

$$customers_{\text{month\_n}} = customers_{\text{start}} + 100 \times n = 50 + 6 * 100 = 650$$
people in the network after 6 months.

20. Company Z has constant Free Cash Flows (FCF). What is the DCF formula until year n?

This is a good example of geometric progression:

$$\sum_{k=1}^{n} \frac{FCF}{(1+w)^k} = FCF \times \sum_{k=1}^{n} \frac{1}{(1+w)^k}; \text{with } w = WACC$$

$$\rightarrow \text{ initial term } FCF; \text{ scale factor } q = \frac{1}{1+w}$$

21. Find the number of movies above which it becomes more interesting to pay a USD 200 membership fee to access any movies, rather than simply pay a USD 15 ticket without membership.

$$200 = 15 \times x \rightarrow x = \frac{200}{15} \approx 13.3 \text{ movies are needed to break-even.}$$

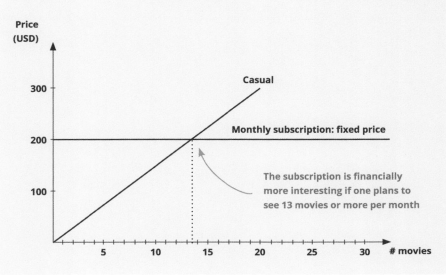

QUANT SOLUTIONS – NICE TO KNOW QUANT
STATISTICS AND PROBABILITY

22. 40% of people have hypertension. 20% diabetes. 10% have both. What is the probability of having either hypertension or diabetes?

$$P(A \text{ or } B) = P(A) + P(B) - P(A \text{ and } B)$$

→ **40% + 20% – 10% = 50%** people have one or both of these two conditions.

23. An airline company noticed that 10% of its customers do not show up for their flight. It decides to accept up to 98 bookings for 95 seats. If 98 bookings were made on a flight, what is the formula giving the probability that everyone showing up gets a seat?

$$P(X \leq 95) = 1 - P(X = 98, 97 \text{ or } 96) \text{ with}$$
$$P(X = k) = \binom{n}{k} \times p^k \times (1-p)^{n-k} \text{ , with n = 98 and p = 0.9}$$

Note: with a scientific calculator or the BINOM.DIST function in Excel, we can easily calculate each of these probabilities and find that the sum is equal to approx. 0.2%, meaning the likelihood for all passengers showing up to have a seat is approximately 99.8%.

24. A TelCo company sells bundles of 3 products out of its 5 products.
How many bundles are there?

Here the order does not matter.
Assuming there is no repetition (3 distinct products), we can calculate the binomial coefficient:

$$\binom{5}{3} = \frac{5!}{(3!*2!)} = \frac{120}{12} = 10$$

CORE KNOWLEDGE OVERVIEW

You will find below a list of the pages you should absolutely master before heading to your first round of interviews.

ABBREVIATIONS

B2B	Business-to-Business
B2C	Business-to-Consumer
BI	Business Intelligence
BP	Business Plan
BU	Business Unit
CAGR	Compound Annual Growth Rate
CAPEX	Capital Expenditure
COGS	Cost Of Goods Sold
CSR	Corporate Social Responsibility
DCF	Discounted Cash Flow
FCF	Free Cash Flows
GMAT	Graduate Management Admission Test
IPO	Initial Public Offering
IRR	Internal Rate of Return
JV	Joint-venture
KPI	Key Performance Indicator
KSF	Key Success Factor
LBO	Leveraged Buy-Out
M&A	Mergers & Acquisition
MBB	McKinsey, Bain, BCG
MBO	Management Buy-Out

MECE	Mutually Exclusive and Collectively Exhaustive
NPV	Net Present Value
PE	Private Equity
P&L	Profit & Loss Statement
PMI	Post Merger Integration
PMO	Program Management Office
PPP	Public-Private Partnership
PST	Problem Solving Test (McKinsey)
R&D	Research & Development
RFP	Request For Proposal
ROA	Return on Assets
ROCE	Return on Capital Employed
ROE	Return on Equity
ROI	Return on Investment
SBS	Strategic Business Segment
SCQ	Situation - Complication - Questions
SME	Subject Matter Expert
STEERCO	Steering Committee
VC	Venture Capital
WACC	Weighted Average Cost of Capital

INDEX (1/3)

INDEX (2/3)

INDEX (3/3)

ABOUT THE AUTHORS

Virgil Baradeau is a former Senior Strategy Manager at Monitor Group/Monitor Deloitte, where he delivered growth strategy projects for multinational companies, primarily in the life sciences and healthcare sector. He is now Partner in charge of Strategy & Analytics for life sciences & healthcare organizations at Greenknowe Advisory, a boutique consultancy.

Virgil was in charge of recruitment at Monitor Paris, working closely with the Managing Partner. In this context, he reviewed the definition of target schools and filtering criteria, screened thousands of applications, defined the on-campus presence strategy, streamlined the recruitment process, and trained Senior Consultants on how to interview junior candidates. He was also part of the recruitment team in Sydney to interview aspiring Managers and Senior Managers.

Virgil holds a MSc in Engineering from Ecole Centrale Lille (France) and a MSc in Strategic Management from HEC Paris (France).

Adeline Chanel is a former strategy senior consultant from Roland Berger Strategy Consultants in Paris. She primarily delivered there Private Equity/Mergers & Acquisitions due diligences, PMI and transformation projects, as well as operations engagements in the retail, fast moving consumer goods and industrials sector. Adeline is now delivering in-house strategy and transformation engagements in the TelCo space.

Adeline was part of the recruitment team at Roland Berger, focusing on interns and consultants recruitment for the Paris office.

Adeline holds a MSc in Engineering from INSA Lyon (France) and a MSc in Strategic Management from HEC Paris (France).

Questions? Feedback? Need support?
Email the authors: contact@stratinterviews.com

Printed in Great Britain
by Amazon